MASSACRE
at Wickenburg

Also by R. Michael Wilson

Frontier Justice in the Wild West
Great Stagecoach Robberies of the Old West
Great Train Robberies of the Old West
Tragic Jack

MASSACRE
at Wickenburg

Arizona's Greatest Mystery

R. Michael Wilson

TWODOT®

GUILFORD, CONNECTICUT
HELENA, MONTANA
AN IMPRINT OF THE GLOBE PEQUOT PRESS

A · T W O D O T® · B O O K

Front cover drawing courtesy of the author's collection. Interior photos are courtesy of the author's collection, except where otherwise noted.

Text design by Lisa Reneson
Map by M. A. Dubé

Library of Congress Cataloging-in-Publication Data
Wilson, R. Michael, 1944-
   Massacre at Wickenburg : Arizona's greatest mystery / R. Michael
Wilson. — 1st ed.
      p. cm.
   Includes bibliographical references and index.
   ISBN-13: 978-0-7627-4453-4
   1. Wickenburg Region (Ariz.)—History—19th century. 2. Massacres—
Arizona—Wickenburg Region—History—19th century. 3. Apache
Indians—Wars. 4. Mohave Indians—Wars. I. Title.
   F819.W44W55 2007
   979.1'7304—dc22
                                            2007033891
Manufactured in the United States of America
First Edition/First Printing

CONTENTS

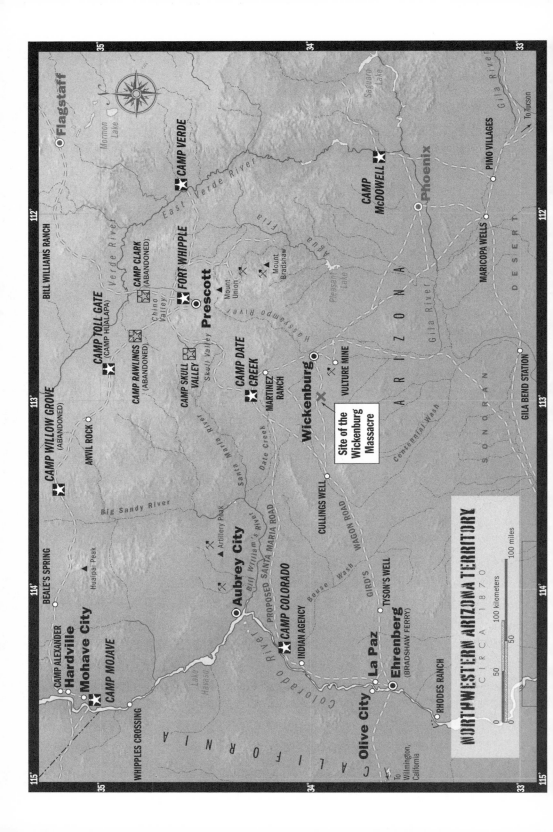

NORTHWESTERN ARIZONA TERRITORY
CIRCA 1870

Flagstaff

Mormon Lake

BILL WILLIAMS RANCH

CAMP VERDE

East Verde River

Verde River

CAMP TOLL GATE
(CAMP HUALAPA)

CAMP CLARK
(ABANDONED)

FORT WHIPPLE

Chino Valley

Prescott

Mount Union

Mount Bradshaw

CAMP WILLOW GROVE
(ABANDONED)

CAMP RAWLINGS
(ABANDONED)

ANVIL ROCK

CAMP SKULL VALLEY

Skull Valley

CAMP DATE CREEK

MARTINEZ RANCH

Date Creek

Pleasant Lake

Agua Fria

Hassayampa River

CAMP McDOWELL

Phoenix

Saguaro Lake

Gila River

PIMO VILLAGES

To Tucson

MARICOPA WELLS

DESERT

Santa Maria River

Big Sandy River

BEALE'S SPRING

Huaipai Peak

Artillery Peak

Bill William's River

AUBREY CITY

Wickenburg

VULTURE MINE

Site of the Wickenburg Massacre

CULLINGS WELL

A R I Z O N A

Gila River

S O N O R A N

GILA BEND STATION

DESERT

MARICOPA WELLS

CAMP ALEXANDER

Hardville

Mohave City

CAMP MOJAVE

WHIPPLES CROSSING

C A L I F O R N I A

Lake Havasu

Colorado River

CAMP COLORADO

INDIAN AGENCY

PROPOSED SANTA MARIA ROAD

Bouse Wash

WAGON ROAD

GIRD'S

TYSON'S WELL

La Paz

Ehrenberg
(BRADSHAW FERRY)

Olive City

RHODES RANCH

To Willmington, California

Centennial Wash

50   100 kilometers

0   50   100 miles

Chapter 1

The Camp Grant Massacre

In the mid- to late-nineteenth century, easterners chastised the Anglos of southwestern America for their poor treatment of the noble savage. Eastern newspapers were the voice of America, and eastern politicians set Indian policy for the nation. The easterners' predisposition regarding sympathy for the poor, trodden southwestern Indian was intensified by an incident that occurred in late April 1871.

It was December 1870 when Lt. Royal Emerson Whitman[1] arrived at Camp Grant (sixty miles northeast of Tucson at the outlet of the Arivaipa Creek that flows into the San Pedro River) to command Company H of the Third Cavalry. Word of his arrival spread, and within a few weeks a contingent of Gilleño-Apache squaws arrived to verify the dispensation of their food allotments, take measure of the new commander, and reconnoiter the camp. Reassured by what they learned, they stayed several days before leaving. They returned within a week to inform the lieutenant that their chief would come within two days.

As promised, Chief Eskiminzin, "Ol' Skimmy," arrived with a

contingent of twenty-five warriors. A few had old rifles; the rest carried bows and arrows. The chief announced that his tribe was tired of fighting and wanted only to live on their land in peace. Ol' Skimmy offered their weapons in trade for seeds and tools. Lieutenant Whitman scrutinized each warrior carefully. Chief Eskiminzin looked well fed and in good health for his advanced age, so the offer to surrender and move onto the reservation was not motivated by a need for food or shelter. The lieutenant accepted the chief's offer to trade for farming implements. Chief Eskiminzin told him that he would bring in three hundred men, women, and children but that it could take several weeks to gather them.

Lieutenant Whitman immediately wrote to Gen. George Stoneman to advise him of the pending arrival of this large number of Indians and to ask for orders. Once the Indians began to arrive, their numbers quickly grew to over five hundred. They included Indians from other area tribes. Lieutenant Whitman did not receive a reply from General Stoneman, so he wrote again asking for instructions. His second letter was returned after several weeks, because he failed to write a brief explanation of its contents on the outer envelope as required by army policy.

Whitman had no directions but a large number of Indians who had to be fed and cared for. He arranged for the Indians to work for local ranchers harvesting barley. The agreement provided that the Indians would be compensated with tools, food, and some money. At first the citizens of Tucson praised Lieutenant Whitman's efforts. However, when raids and killings in the Santa Cruz and San Pedro Valleys increased, praise quickly turned to criticism. This compelled William S. Oury, one of the more outspoken critics of Indian policy, to encourage Tucson's Committee for Public Safety to speak with General Stoneman. This was the first the general heard of the growing problem.

The general, in the face of vehement disapproval, reminded the committee that President Grant and Gen. William T. Sherman ordered the adoption of a policy of persuasion and kindness, and that they encouraged Christianization of the Indians. General Stoneman sent the delegation back to Tucson with a veiled statement of support, suggesting, "Certainly you must do what you can to protect your own lives."

The general found himself in an untenable position. In the East he was being criticized for being insensitive, even brutal, toward the Indians; locally he was criticized because he couldn't control them. His solution was to send Capt. Frank Stanwood to Camp Grant to assume command over Whitman and Company H. Stanwood was given this injunction: "Your wards, I understand there are more than five hundred Apache there now, will be considered prisoners of war so that the Army is authorized to feed them. You will treat those Indians who are deserving with all the sensitivity and compassion the Dutch Reformed Church demands, but you will continue patrols. I want aggressive pursuit of those Indians responsible for any depredations in the territory. You must administer appropriate punishment to the Indians responsible."

By the time Captain Stanwood arrived at Camp Grant, many of the Indians residing there had left and settled at the rancheria five miles north of Camp Grant on Arivaipa Creek. Water was sufficient at the new settlement, and the Indians were determined to make a serious effort at farming the land. Stanwood, satisfied with the organization of Camp Grant and the relocation of the Indians, quickly turned command back to Whitman. Captain Stanwood decided his most pressing need was to lead an extended patrol to become familiar with the terrain and to pursue raiders in the Santa Cruz and San Pedro Valleys. He was particularly concerned with capturing those Indians who struck in the area around San Xavier del Bac on April 10. Captain Stanwood left Camp Grant on April 24, 1871.

Meanwhile William Oury continued to encourage vigilantism in Tucson. He met with Jesus Maria Elias, who represented the Mexican population. They agreed to combine forces in a punitive expedition. John Vesberg, one of Oury's vigilantes, suggested that the Papago Indians would join the posse if their chief, Francisco Galerita, was asked.

It was a moonless night on April 28 when the vigilante group slipped out of Tucson. The men regrouped at the Rillito River. Elias brought forty-eight men. Oury arrived a bit later with only five of the eighty men he had promised. He explained that he deployed men along routes to Camp Grant so that they would turn back those who might try to warn Whitman, now perceived as an "Indian lover" who would deploy his troops against the punitive party. With too few men they almost gave up the plan, but when ninety-four Papago Indians arrived led by Chief Francisco, the plan proceeded.

Though Oury failed to provide the men he had promised, he brought a wagonload of supplies, arms, and ammunition. The Mexicans outnumbered the Whites and the Papago's weren't allowed to vote, so by default Elias was elected leader. With a force of 150 well-armed men at his command, Elias departed for the Apache rancheria located above Camp Grant.

It was an hour before sunrise on Sunday morning when the vigilante group arrived at the Apache rancheria. The band of Apaches had become accustomed to the treachery of the Whites and Mexicans, and so a man and a woman were placed on lookout. When the attackers arrived the lookouts were preoccupied with a game of cards. Chief Francisco sent four braves to dispatch the guards while the Whites and Mexicans moved up the left bank of the Arivaipa Creek to a bluff above the encampment. There they waited until the Papagos disposed of the guards and the signal was given to attack.

As agreed, no guns were used in the initial assault. Each of the

150 men rushed the wickiups (brush huts common in that region) with a club in one hand and a knife in the other. While many of the Apaches fled, 135 old men, women, and children were clubbed and hacked to death in a few minutes of carnage. The attackers herded together twenty-eight small children and took them as prisoners, to later be distributed among families and raised as their own. There were no warrior-aged men to be found in the rancheria that morning.

Lieutenant Whitman received word of the attack much too late to send aid. He took his troopers to the rancheria and found dead Indians scattered everywhere. Chief Eskiminzin returned to the rancheria just as the troopers were burying the dead. The chief swore he would not break his faith with Whitman but pleaded with him to make every effort to find the missing children. Whitman tried every means at his disposal, including a reward for information, but to no avail. He could not identify the murderers nor find even one of the children.

In late May a group of foraging Apaches surprised a troop of cavalry troopers, and the soldiers fired at the Indians. With this incident Chief Eskiminzin finally lost faith. He told Lieutenant Whitman that there was no hope for peace and led his people far away from Camp Grant.

The massacre at Camp Grant had outraged the nation, including the president for whom the camp was named. At President Grant's behest, U.S. District Attorney C. W. C. Rowell arrived in Tucson on September 15, 1871. Rowell's investigation proved successful in identifying the guilty parties. When the U.S. grand jury met in early September, they ignored the urging of Rowell to indict those responsible for the massacre. However, they were not prepared to defy him when he let it be known that nothing less than an indictment would prevent declaration of federal martial law in the territory. One hundred men were indicted by the grand jury in late September for the massacre at Camp Grant, and another indictment was handed down for Chief Eskiminzin for the murder of Charles McKenney.

McKenney was among a select minority of 1870s Arizonians. He liked and trusted the Indians and was sympathetic to their plight. When Eskiminzin led his people away from Camp Grant, away from the lands around the Aravaipa River that had been their home for centuries, he announced: "We will stop at the farm of my good friend, Charles McKenney." McKenney was surprised to find hundreds of Indians in front of his home. He invited his long-time friend to supper and asked, "Skimmy, what has happened? Are you breaking out?"

Chief Eskiminzin didn't need to tell McKenney about the massacre. It had been the topic of discussion and speculation throughout the nation for nearly a month. Instead, he told him about his decision to move his people to a safer place. The afternoon passed in idle chatter. McKenney had to carry most of the conversation, because the chief was more quiet than usual. McKenney couldn't help but express his concern for the chief and his people, and he apologized for the actions of the white soldiers. McKenney served an early supper and afterward the two men sat for awhile, sipped coffee, and enjoyed a smoke together. It was then time for the tribe to move on.

The days had grown longer and sunlight still remained for the Indians to move onward toward the mountains. The chief rose, grasped the hand of his friend, and placed it between both his hands. He learned this technique from other white men and understood it to be a symbol of extreme sincerity. He told McKenney, "You are a good and honest man. A true friend to me and to my people." McKenney was embarrassed and thanked him profusely for the compliment. "Please come back any time, and soon. You, too, are a good friend and I will miss not having you nearby." Suddenly, Chief Eskiminzin dropped his friend's hand, pulled his pistol, and shot

McKenney through the heart. He moved quickly and shot true so that his friend would not have time to be afraid or to feel pain.

The chief then walked out of the farmhouse to face his people. The entire tribe had risen to their feet at the sound of the gunshot. They had not known about their chief's plan and feared it was he who had been slain. Chief Eskiminzin called his warriors to him and showed them the body of his friend. He told them, "I have done this to show you that there can be no friendship with the Anglos." One young warrior asked, "Why did you kill a friend when there are so many enemies to kill?" The chief explained, "Any coward can kill his enemy, but it takes a brave man to kill his friend."

At the October term of the U.S. District Court an indictment for murder was found against one hundred of the Camp Grant vigilantes. At the arraignment five of the defendants appeared in person, pleaded not guilty, and posted bail in the sum of ten thousand dollars for their appearance at the upcoming December term. The remaining ninety-five defendants appeared by proxy to the satisfaction of the court.

In December, ninety-nine defendants appeared in person to answer the charge; only one man was absent and unintentionally so. In *United States v. Sidney R. DeLong, et al.*, U.S. Attorney Rowell presented the case for the prosecution while James E. McCaffrey and Granville Oury, brother of one defendant, presented the defense. Judge John Titus presided over the five-day trial. Jury deliberations lasted only nineteen minutes before Jury Foreman Charles T. Hayden read the not guilty verdict acquitting all ninety-nine defendants.

Who would have imagined that within a month a single Indian depredation would deteriorate the resolve to protect the southwestern tribes and cause the eastern press and politicians to supplant sympathy with a call for stern retribution.

Chapter 2

The Travelers

On a crisp, clear Sunday morning, November 4, 1871, seven passengers assembled at the Prescott,[2] Arizona, depot of the Arizona Stage Company.[3] They were immediately bound for Wickenburg[4] and then destinations westward. Their coach was a celerity or "mud" wagon drawn by a team of four horses.

Peter M. Hamel, William George Salmon, and Frederick Wadsworth Loring had just completed an eight-month trek with Dr. Cochrane's contingent of Lt. George M. Wheeler's[5] survey team. All three were bound for San Francisco, home to Hamel and Salmon and the embarkation point for Loring who was returning home to Boston. Frederick Shoholm, another passenger, had just sold his interest in a Prescott jewelry business and was traveling to San Francisco to board a steamship. His final destination was home to Philadelphia by way of Panama. Charles S. Adams had left his employment with W. Bichard & Company because of an illness in his family and was en route home to San Francisco where his wife and three children lived. Mollie Sheppard had been a successful courtesan in Prescott for several years and had recently liquidated her holdings to travel west to San Francisco where she planned to board a steamer bound for Panama City. William Kruger was employed as clerk for the army's quartermaster in the Arizona Territory and was en route to Ehrenberg. Kruger was the only passenger not bound for San Francisco via Los Angeles. In Wickenburg the group picked up an eighth passenger, Aaron Barnett.

The road from Prescott to Wickenburg had been improved and shortened thanks to prominent Arizona pioneer Charles Baldwin Genung, though the new road was still a work in progress. The new route, by way of Antelope Creek Station, would bring the travelers to the stage company's main station in Wickenburg after midnight, allowing them several hours sleep before leaving for Ehrenberg[6] at 7 a.m. the following day.

The morning of November 5 was much like the morning before, clear and crisp, but it promised to warm considerably by midday. Civil twilight, the period of brightening sky which precedes sunrise, began at 6:20 a.m. with sunrise at 6:54 a.m. The moon was waning, being only four days past full, and along with a multitude of stars had lighted the previous evening quite effectively. The moon had risen at 11:25 p.m. the night before and would set at 1:50 p.m.

Driver "Dutch" John Lance[7] was loading the baggage in the coach as the eastbound mail buckboard set out for Phoenix and Tucson at 6:00 a.m. Lance called for boarding and the coach left on schedule. Charles Adams and Frederick Loring elected to ride atop, the other passengers within the coach. Barnett forgot something in Wickenburg, so he dismounted a few miles outside of Wickenburg and walked back to town.

It was common practice to choose the smoothest existing course of travel for wagons, and it was the rare water of the desert that naturally found those courses. Water, over the years, etched washes and arroyos into the sand and rocks of the desert landscape, creating smooth trails for wagons and riders. One such trail was the La Paz Road. The excellent road conditions of the La Paz Road required only a four-horse team to pull a large coach. Sol's Wash on La Paz Road flowed southeast into the Hassayampa River and passed about a half mile north of the Trinidad House, the main stage depot for the Arizona Stage Company in 1871.

A westbound stage leaving Wickenburg would enter the wash from the northwest and then turn due west. The trace intersected with Gird's Wagon Road near where Charles Culling dug his well[8] thirty-six miles west of Wickenburg. The wash then continued west toward the town of Ehrenberg, which was established when the town of La Paz[9] failed. Early one morning in March 1868 the residents of La Paz awoke to find that the fickle Colorado River had changed course overnight and the town was no longer situated on its east bank. Most of the townspeople moved south approximately five miles, resituated on the river's east bank, and named the new town Ehrenberg. On the morning of November 5, 1871, the Concord-style stagecoach was on the Wickenburg to Ehrenberg run on the La Paz Road.

Large-model coaches were rarely used on rough terrain. The "mud" or celerity wagon, or an even more basic spring-supported wagon such as a buckboard, was more suitable for rough terrain. There are some historians, however, who have tried to piece together the history of stagecoaches and have suggested that there were no Concord wagons or coaches in Arizona in the early 1870s. The following article from the October 2, 1869, edition of the *Miner* (Prescott, Arizona Territory)[10] suggests the contrary:

Stage Line—James Grant,[11] the pioneer stage man of this section, arrived here Tuesday afternoon last from California in a brand new Concord wagon drawn by six mules in which, also, came the mail and six passengers whose names are as follows: Wm. M. Buffum of Campbell & Buffum, Prescott; Miss W. Wilburn; Mrs Jennie Wells; M. Simonsen; Lt. Ledgewood and Mr. Saunders. As will be seen by advertisement published elsewhere, Mr. Grant proposes to run a weekly line of stages between Prescott and La Paz to connect with that of Nobles & Waters on the other end of the route between Prescott and San Bernardino, California. We doubt not the enterprise will be well sustained, and it ought to be.

A Concord-style coach with a four-horse team can travel eight to nine miles per hour when not pressed for speed and when the roads are level and in good condition. By 8:00 a.m. the coach from Wickenburg was only eight miles from town. The trip had continued uneventfully until driver Lance yelled out an alarm. The stagecoach was being attacked from three sides—the left or south side, the front, and the rear. To this day, theories abound as to who committed the murders of six men and wounded a woman and a seventh man eight miles west of Wickenburg, Arizona, that fateful morning. Suspects included . . .

the Yavapai Indians from the reservation at Camp Date Creek[12] (this tribe was better known in Arizona as the Apache-Mojave tribe, though they were neither Apache nor Mojave Indians);

a Mexican gang headed by the notorious outlaw Joaquin Barbe and alleged to include Ramon Cordova, Trini Gonzales, Ernando Hernandez, Juan Reval, and five unnamed Mexicans;

a combination of the aforementioned Indians and Mexicans. The Indians in this case are nearly always characterized as renegades or "broncos" since, in 1871, few Indians would ever raid with Mexicans;

a similar combination of Mexicans and Indians backed by white men who were involved in the "Indian Rings"—influential businessmen and government employees who prospered when Indian troubles occurred;

white men from Prescott who were intent on robbing passenger Mollie Sheppard, a prominent and successful prostitute who had sold her business in Prescott; and

William Kruger and Mollie Sheppard, the surviving passengers, who killed and robbed the other travelers, buried the loot in the desert, and then wounded each other before walking westward toward Culling's Well.

By 1871 Arizona Territory settlers had been plagued by Indian hostilities for decades, but that was just a continuation of the depredations the tribes had conducted against Mexicans for three centuries and against each other for years. San Francisco's *Daily Alta California* newspaper described the plight of Arizona's settlers: "At least five hundred men have been killed and a large number of them were horribly tortured and those who are left, after fighting for years to hold the country, find themselves in poverty and are looked upon as barbarians."

The same newspaper, in a later article, provided examples of the torture: "He [the Indian] is inventive in his means of torture. Women are often made captives and subjected to a life worse than death. Children are placed on spears and roasted before a slow fire, and writhe in misery until life is extinct. Men are hanged by the feet and a slow fire kindled at the head, and gashed with knives and pierced with arrows until death gives relief."

Before the massacre eastern sympathy was with "the noble redman." Newspapers and politicians found every reason to condemn the settlers of the Arizona Territory and criticize their continuous warring with the Indians. The Camp Grant Indian killings in April 1871 provided the easterners a *cause celebre*. Peace commissioners were sent west to parley with the Indians and to set aside large tracts of land for them and to provide for their needs. As quickly as the first commissioner Vincent Colyer made his rounds and issued his promises on behalf of the government, the Indians were off their reservations raiding the surrounding countryside. Colyer traveled west on the stage from Wickenburg to Ehrenberg in early October, the same stage attacked a month later, to report his successes to President Grant.

Sympathies would have remained with the Indians of the Arizona Territory except that one of the men murdered on November 5 was a promising young writer from Boston, a recent Harvard graduate, who was a correspondent for *Appleton's Journal*. At the loss of one of their own, an easterner slaughtered by the hand of an Indian, the tone changed. The *Daily Alta California* reported in their Christmas Eve 1871 edition, "There is a marked change in the tone of the Eastern press upon the Indian question. Many of the leading papers, finding they had been imposed upon by Mr. Colyer in his report of affairs in Arizona, have turned upon him with much severity. The Boston newspapers, since the death of young Loring, have discovered that the Apache is not the amiable and peace-loving creature Mr. Colyer would make him out to be."

The Wickenburg massacre was an important turning point in relations with the tribes of the Southwest, because it changed the image of the Indians among the easterners who made policy. As a result of the massacre, a philosophy was adopted that the Indians would be thoroughly whipped and subjugated before they could seek and maintain a lasting peace. Eastern sentiment had changed to "more sword and less Bible."

The question remained, why would Indians in the Southwest attack a stagecoach, kill six men, and then steal very little? The items left behind served as an important element in the proposition that the attack was made by Mexicans rather than Indians. Many of the items left behind were highly prized by the Indians—items such as horses, colorful shawls, jewelry, and a leather harness.

If plunder was not their intention, then what was? One week after the massacre, the *Daily Alta California* reported, "We can get no particulars as to the cause of the attack, further than a supposition that it was in retaliation for the shooting of an Indian recently. The supposition is strengthened by the fact that the Indians took nothing from the stage." On November 16, 1871, the *Miner* reported, "Parties are in pursuit of the savages, who seem to have been incited by revenge rather than hopes of plunder." Based upon the evidence, revenge seems like the most plausible explanation for the attack.

Further, the target of the attack may have been one or more of the three men from the Wheeler expedition: Loring, Hamel, or Salmon. All three men had been in Dr. Cochrane's contingent of the party surveying the Southwest. Loring provided accounts of the progress of the expedition in several published articles.

The party was in Arizona when Loring reported on Tuesday, August 24 that Death Valley was behind them. Their guide, a "mountain man," had proven to be a fraud and abandoned the party three days earlier. Loring wrote in response to his leaving: "I sing . . . to the great delight of an Indian—'a heap good Indian,' of course, who is stealing 'muck-a-muck' from us daily." The Indian he was referring to appears to have joined the party after it left Death Valley and was probably an Arizona Indian, since it seems unlikely they would tolerate a thief, even a petty thief, if he could not contribute something valuable to future travel. It may even be supposed, from the events that followed, that he was a Yavapai Indian from the reservation at Date Creek.

When Loring was in Wickenburg he was unarmed. He was offered a pistol but declined, and stated that he was not concerned because, as he put it, "I have not seen an Indian in Arizona." However, his article shows that he not only saw an Indian but had been traveling with one. It would be purely conjecture to say that a young, naive easterner would, upon arriving on the wild western frontier, immediately arm himself to dispel the "greenhorn" image. It is possible that it was Loring who shot the Indian thief, then refused to carry a pistol and denied ever seeing an Indian. If it was Loring who killed the Indian for whom revenge was sought, then the Date Creek murderers had accomplished their purpose.

BULLET WOUNDS TALLIED

The stagecoach in use on November 5, 1871, was reported to be a Concord model capable of carrying twenty-one passengers, nine inside and twelve on top. By 1871 "Concord" had become a generic term for a variety of coaches and wagons. Therefore, even if this particular coach was not made by the Abbot & Downing Company[13] of Concord, New Hampshire, evidence shows that it was a wooden-sided enclosed coach of similar design and size.

Several western carriage works were producing coaches that resembled the Concord. The body of a Concord stagecoach, or counterfeit Concord, is made of wood and supported on thick leather through braces that allow the body to "rock like a cradle" and thus absorb the movement caused by the roadway. High-back bench seats in the coach face each other and between those seats is a backless bench for passengers to sit facing either direction.

Frederick Loring and Charles Adams joined stagecoach driver Lance on top. Wounds inflicted upon these men suggest that Charles Adams, with two wounds to his lower back, sat on the left or south side of the coach nearest the attackers. Frederick Loring sat in the center and received wounds to his head and upper torso. Lance sat in the driver's seat on the right side of the coach, a position from which he could control the horses and manage the brake. Lance received wounds to his head, chest, and arm. Though it has occasionally been suggested that Loring was seated on the right, it seems highly improbable that an experienced stagecoach driver traveling an unfamiliar trail would relinquish the brake to a "green" easterner. Further, Lance's wounds substantiate the conclusion that he was seated on the right.

Within the coach Mollie Sheppard was seated on the left facing rear, which placed her right arm against the wooden side of the coach. This positioning is substantiated by the wound to her right arm that contained wooden splinters from the coach's body.

Directly across from Ms. Sheppard was Aaron Barnett. Barnett was a prominent Wickenburg businessman. Fortunately for him, Mr. Barnett dismounted the coach a few miles west of town when he realized he had "forgotten something important" and walked back to Wickenburg. His forgetfulness saved his life, and he played no part in the events of the massacre. However, when the inquest jury convened on November 6, 1871, Barnett's name appears as a member of the jury.

William Kruger was seated in the center of the rear-facing seat next to Ms. Sheppard. To his left against the north window was William George Salmon. Across from Salmon was Peter M. Hamel. To Hamel's left, in the center of the forward-facing seat, was Frederick Shoholm. This interior positioning allowed the four men to engage in a card game of "freeze-out."

It was not uncommon for passengers to remove their side arms for comfort's sake and place them beneath the cushions of their seat. At the moment of the attack, the center bench was being used as a table for the card game. Mollie Sheppard's fur cape was used as a table throw. The fur cape was later recovered by Ms. Sheppard and bore evidence to the ferocity of the attack—nine bullet holes penetrated the cape.

It has never been contested that the first alarm of the attack was a shout from driver Lance: "Apaches! Apaches! Apaches!" The alarm was preceded by a simultaneous volley of shots, and almost immediately thereafter a second volley of shots was fired. As quickly as it began, the fusillades ceased. Killed outright were Shoholm and Lance. Loring and Adams were seriously wounded and unable to flee, and they were murdered where they lay. Salmon had received wounds to his stomach but still fought bravely before being killed. Hamel may have been unhurt, circumstances suggesting that he met his attackers head-on and battled them bravely before being killed. Hamel may have sacrificed himself so that Ms. Sheppard could escape, the slightly wounded Kruger with her.

Inspection of the stagecoach revealed seventeen individual entry holes in the wooden body of the coach. On December 9, 1871, the *San Bernardino* (California) *Guardian* newspaper reported the number of bullet holes: "THE STAGE—On his way to Prescott two weeks ago, Judge C. A. Tweed was invited to examine the stage recently captured by Indians near Wickenburg. From the manner in which it is perforated in every direction, the Judge is surprised that even one of the passengers should have escaped. He counted seventeen bullet holes—the greatest number of which were in the sides and at a proper elevation to perfect the work of murder—and the work was pretty effectually accomplished."

After the massacre, the coach was taken out of service. The *Miner* reported that it was "cursed, with all stage drivers positively refusing to drive on it." When the stage line moved its headquarters to Prescott in 1892, the coach was driven there by the superintendent and left in a storage yard. In 1893 the *Miner* reported that the coach was still in W. J. Mulvenon's old stage yard where it sat deteriorating. From 1892 to 1900, Prescott was plagued by several devastating fires. It was probably during one of these blazes that the remnants of the Wickenburg massacre stagecoach were burned to ashes.

In accounting for the total rounds fired during the attack, the three men riding on top of the coach each received at least two bullet wounds. John Lance was shot in the arm, the chest, and the head, but it is possible that the arm and chest wound were from a single bullet. Frederick Loring was shot through the chest, which punctured a lung. He was also shot in the eye and in the temple, though it is likely that those wounds were an entry and exit wound caused by a single bullet. Charles Adams was shot twice in the back, one bullet severing his spine and paralyzing him from the neck down.

It was reported that a lance thrust to the chest was what killed Loring. There are two accounts of Adams's final death wound: the first account suggests his throat was cut while the second states he was shot in the head at close range with his own pistol. The inquest jury does not mention Charles Adams's throat being cut, an omission that supports the latter account.

The near-lead horse, fore left, died from three bullet wounds. The off-lead horse, fore right, suffered from a single bullet wound. It is possible that one bullet may have struck both horses by passing through or ricocheting off the near leader into the off leader.

The final minimum tally of bullet wounds to the coach—which includes the wounds to those inside (seventeen), the wounds to the men seated outside (six), and the horses (three)—is twenty-six. Thus, no less than thirteen shooters could have inflicted twenty-six wounds from long arms in two volleys. The maximum number accountable by visible wounds is twenty-nine, requiring a minimum of fifteen shooters. This raises two major issues of contention.

One issue is that the coordination of the two volleys suggests that an additional person may have been present to signal the firing of the first volley, or that there were at least fourteen attackers. The second issue is that firing ceased even after it became clear that people remained alive, indicating that the attackers were out of ammunition. This conclusion withstands a further analysis, since nine attackers reportedly chased William Kruger and Mollie Sheppard into the desert but were kept at bay when Kruger brandished or fired his pistol. However, it is possible that a single pursuer with a long arm and a few rounds of ammunition could have dispatched both survivors in a few moments without being placed within range of Kruger's handgun. It is clear, therefore, that the attackers had no more ammunition for their rifles. Mexicans and Whites had access to all the ammunition they wanted while Indians were denied access to ammunition.

The positioning of the attackers has also proven controversial with some historians placing the attackers on both sides of the coach and at the front and rear. However, it seems evident that the attackers were all on the south side of the coach, on high ground, and spread out at several points along the trail. In this most likely scenario, the firing from the front and rear would have come from attackers at the furthest perimeter points while the greatest concentration of attackers was directly opposite the side of the coach.

The wounds inflicted suggest that the attackers were positioned to the south. Shoholm was seated south of Hamel and was killed outright while Hamel was unhurt. Sheppard received a wound to her right arm, which lay against the south-facing wall of the coach. No wounds seem to have come from the north as they were all inflicted to the front or rear.

The attackers fired at the lead horses to bring them down and stop the coach, but only the near-lead horse, on the left or south, was killed. The off-lead horse on the north side received only a minor wound, recovered, and remained in service for more than a decade after the attack. To the north the ground was flat and it would have been far more difficult for the perpetrators to hide effectively. In a letter posted December 9, 1871, Kruger stated: "Well, in about six minutes of terrible suspense I saw the Indians slowly creeping toward the stage. I counted and saw plainly fifteen Indians."

Finally, if the attackers had been positioned north of the coach, it is unlikely that Kruger and Sheppard could have so easily exited from the coach on the north side and escaped west into the dry arroyo.

POSITION AND HARNESS OF THE STAGECOACH

In the "Corrected Account of the Massacre" published in the *Miner* newspaper on November 18, 1871, members of the pursuit posse reported: "Judging from the indication after killing the passengers, something scared the Indians causing them to leave in hot haste—scattering in different directions."

When the first rescue party from Wickenburg arrived on the scene, the stagecoach had been turned around to face east. As well, the harness had been stacked on the doubletrees and crossbars "as if by an old hostler," three live horses had been turned loose, and the dead horse was lying at the rear of the coach. This manipulation of the scene, it was later argued, was proof that non-Indians were responsible and that they had set the scene as it was first discovered by the rescuers. However, eighty years later an explanation was provided.

Historical records predating 1950 do not suggest how the army was notified of the massacre. It was in August 1950 that Elmer Ball, great grandson of pioneer freighter Wright H. Ball,[14] answered these questions when he published his grandfather's story in *Desert Magazine*. According to W. H. Ball's memoirs, teamsters were traveling east from Wilmington, California, that Sunday and had been on the trail several months. They were nearing Wickenburg when, at about noon on November 5, 1871, the teamsters came upon a smoldering stagecoach and six dead men.

Ball reported that the teamsters tried to leave the evidence relatively uncontaminated. However, in turning loose the horses—the only humane thing they could do under the circumstances—they inadvertently turned the coach around and stacked the harness in the customary manner. Ball then explained that his grandfather informed the commanding officer at Camp Date Creek of the massacre. By doing so he hoped to avoid any Indians that might be awaiting their arrival further along a trail that had proven popular for Indian attacks upon freighters. Based on the information provided by Ball, it was the hard-bitten teamsters approaching the scene that set the Indians to flight, and it was the teamsters that turned the coach, released the horses, stacked the harness, and brought word to the army.

Special Order No. 120 was issued early Monday morning, November 6 by Post Adjutant Lt. Fred H. E. Ebstein.[15] The order read:

> Hqtrs. Camp Date Creek, A.T.
> November 6, 1871
>
> I . . . Captain Charles Meinhold[16] 3rd Cavalry, with Lieut. Simpson[17] with 20 men of his troop will proceed at once to the point in the La Paz Road where the mail stage was attacked yesterday and ascertain the particulars connected with the attack and by what parties it was made.
>
> Should Captain Meinhold deem it essential for the proper prosecution of this inquiry to employ a trailer, he is authorized to do so.
>
> By order of Captain R. F. O'Beirne[18]
> 21st Infantry Commanding
> Fred H. E. Ebstein
> 2nd Lieut. 21st Infantry
> Post Adjutant

Capt. Richard Fitzgerald O'Beirne, commanding Camp Date Creek, wrote to the Assistant Adjutant General at Prescott on November 6, 1871:

Sir:

A report reached me at 8 o'clock this morning that the stage which left for Wickenburg A. T. for La Paz yesterday was attacked about seven miles from the former place. Six of the passengers were killed and two wounded. From the statement made to me I am led to believe that the attack was made by parties seeking plunder as evidence of this it is said that the mail bags were cut open and registered letters stolen. Valises and other packages were cut open and a portion of their contents taken. The pockets of the murdered men were turned inside out while blankets, some of bright colors, were not touched, neither were the animals pertaining to the mail coach.

I have sent Captain Meinhold with a detachment of his troop to examine into the affair and the surgeon of post to attend to the wounded.

> I am sir,
> Very respectfully,
> Your obedient svt.,
> R. F. O'Beirne
> Captain 21st Infantry
> Commanding post

Captain Meinhold left Camp Date Creek with twenty troopers. First Lt. Joseph H. Lawson[19] was left in command of the remainder of Company B. There is no record indicating which troopers went with Captain Meinhold, but the detachment probably consisted of at least two of his seven sergeants: John K. Foley, Francois Jourdain, Charles Witzman, Michael Hooban, Charles K. Gardner, William Andrews, and Leroy H. Vokes. He also probably took along two corporals from his complement of four: John Fry, Charles Hawksworth, William Huber, and Charles Anderson. Additionally, he probably took sixteen privates from his complement of thirty-eight:

Andrew Archer	William Ashby
Charles Austin	James Birdfall
William Chapman	Maurice Connell
John DeVoy	James Fisher
John I. Gordon	John M. Gordon
James Haigh	Frank Hatchcock
John Hensell	William Irvine
William Johnson	Henry Kelly
John Kennedy	John Kirkpatrick
Henry Kistner	Max Leibler
Samuel Long	John Lewis
John Malone	John Moriarty
John McClain	Francis Olliver
William Pattison	Thaddeus Pendleton
Ambrose Quigley	Patrick Rourke
Richard Shannahan	George Stickney
William Strayer	Walter Tanner
Thomas Taylor	Charles Timm
Royal Tyler	John Walsh

Captain Meinhold's detachment arrived at Wickenburg Monday evening. Less than a week later, headquarters responded to Captain O'Beirne's special order. The response is important because it shows

Gen. George Crook's[20] interest in this event from the beginning. Capt. Azor H. Nickerson, Adjutant for the General, wrote:

> Sirs:
>
> Referring to the report of the late attack upon the stage near Wickenburg and the massacre of the passengers, the Department Commander directs me to say that he regrets that suitable Indian guides, trailers, were not sent out with Captain Meinhold's command, and that pursuit was not kept up at any sacrifice to determine definitely whether the perpetrators were Indians or Mexican bandits or both.
>
> You will as far as possible remedy the defect by diligent inquiry among the Indians now drawing rations at your post and by such other investigation as you think necessary to determine that matter definitely, and make report thereon without delay.
>
> The importance of a thorough searching investigation of this matter cannot be too earnestly impressed upon you.
>
> > I am sir,
> > Very respectfully,
> > Your Obt. Servant,
> > A. H. Nickerson
> > Captain 23rd Infantry
> > ADC and AAA Genl.

Captain O'Beirne responded on November 29:

> Sir:
>
> In reply to your letter of Nov. 12th concerning the reports made with reference to the attack on the stage near

Wickenburg, on the 4th inst. I have the honor to state that when Captain Meinhold was sent with a portion of his troop to inquire into the affair, he was authorized to employ and did procure a trailer [George Monroe] for the purpose of aiding him in prosecuting the pursuit and I entertaining the belief that he would have succeeded in satisfactorily determining who were the perpetrators of the outrage.

Owing, however, to the fact that there are neither apparhoes [simple pack saddles] nor pack animals at the post, he was only furnished three days rations—these he made last his command for four days.

Frequent inquiries have been made among the Indians drawing rations at this post concerning the affair, but no information has as yet been obtained. Efforts to this end will be continued.

> I am sir,
> Very respectfully,
> Your obedient servant.
> [SD] R. F. O'Beirne
> Captain 21st Infantry
> Commanding post

WEAPONS USED

The *Daily Alta California* on November 16, 1871, reported, "They were well armed with Spencer and Henry rifles." It may be presumed that this determination was made from the easily identifiable bullet casings found at the scene of the attack.

The Spencer carbine was standard arms issue for the frontier's regular cavalry. It has a seven-shot magazine fully enclosed and protected in the butt stock. The cartridge for this cavalry carbine was .50 caliber rim fire. However, unmodified .56 caliber Spencer carbines were sold as surplus at the end of the Civil War and occasionally found their way into Indian hands. The Spencer is operated by throwing the lever forward, dropping the two-piece breechblock, and rolling it backwards on the lever pin. Simultaneously, an expended cartridge is pulled backward by the extractor and ejected rearward from the top of the action if more than one round is to be fired. The Spencer must be manually cocked for each shot.

The Henry rifle has a fifteen-shot tube magazine under the barrel. With a cartridge in the chamber, the Henry can provide its shooter with sixteen rounds, which can be fired in rapid succession. The cartridge for the Henry rifle is .44 caliber rim fire. A round is loaded by operating the lever downward causing the breech bolt to thrust the hammer backwards to full cock position. The follower ejects the casing from the top of the receiver. In firing more than one round, the Henry would eject the previous bullet's casing onto the ground. The Henry rifle, however, has a flaw which could render it a single-shot weapon. Dirt or a dent in the tube magazine, which is exposed and easily damaged in rough use, would jam it. Still, the spent casing would have to be removed and discarded in loading the next round.

The timing of the second volley being so nearly synchronized with the first implies that the attackers' weapons were in working order, and that they were able to operate the lever mechanisms on all long arms in reloading a second round. The number of bullet holes in the coach, the wounds to the men riding atop, and the wounds to the horses indicates a minimum of thirteen attackers. The casings from the first volley would have been ejected so that at least thirteen casings would have been discarded and found at the scene. These distinctive casings would have identified the weapons used. It is possible that some or all of the attackers left the second bullet casing in their weapon, since, by all indications, they had no more ammunition to load after the second volley.

Would Indians have collected the spent casings? Indians lacked the skill, equipment, and material to reload bullet casings. Expended casings had no value and would have been left where they landed during the reloading process, as leaving casings was the practice in all previous and subsequent Indian depredations.

The attackers fired only two cartridges apiece. This may have been all they possessed, but the coincidence of having two or three distinct firearms with the same limitation is unlikely. A more reasonable conclusion is that this limitation was the result of a decision made to conserve ammunition because of the difficulty in obtaining it and only two rounds per man were brought to the scene.

In October 1872 Gen. George Crook issued twenty rifles and twenty rounds of ammunition to Indians whose long arms had been damaged while in the army's care. In response, Charles B. Genung,[21] a well known and respected Arizona pioneer, commented upon the Indians' plight in obtaining ammunition. In his memoirs he stated, "The only way that an Indian could get ammunition was to go to La Paz or Yuma and get some white man to buy it for him." He neglected to mention another method—depredations involving murder and theft.

The Los Angeles *Daily News*, in its January 3, 1872, edition reported that, following the massacre, "The Reservation Indians have also purchased ammunition from the soldiery, giving greenbacks in denominational value of $10 and $20 in payment therefor." If this account is true, the Indians had found yet another source for obtaining ammunition by using money stolen during a robbery to pay a premium price for each bullet.

MOCCASIN TRACKS—STYLE

Capt. Charles Meinhold's report, the only written record of an investigation at the site, states: "I discovered three or four moccasin tracks of the pattern used by the Apache-Mojaves."

Indians walked toe inward and some have suggested that Captain Meinhold was referring to this characteristic in his report. Other historians have dwelt upon the fact that Indian moccasins are round at the toes. However, Captain Meinhold's statement reveals that the moccasin tracks were not just typically Indian, but specifically of a pattern that was distinctive to the Apache-Mojave.

Indians of the Southwest made their moccasins by forming the lower portion upward and lacing them at the top around the foot. This made the edges of their footprints smooth. The Apache-Mojave, or Yavapai Indians, were the exception. They made their moccasins by forming the upper part downward and lacing the upper part to the sole at the base of the foot with a strip of rawhide. Moccasin tracks of the Apache-Mojave, therefore, had a distinctive pattern of rough edges. It was this rough pattern that was identified in an interview with Anna Price (her Indian name was Her Eyes Grey) in *Western Apache Raiding and Warfare*. In the interview, Anna states: "Our men knew they were Yavapai because their moccasins were a little different from ours. They had a habit of sewing the buckskin uppers to the rawhide sole with thin strips of hide. It was possible to see the mark which these seams left in the dirt."

MOCCASIN TRACKS—NUMBER

Captain Meinhold wrote in his report, "I discovered three or four moccasin tracks." He continued, "On the left side . . . I found as many more tracks of the same description," and "About one half mile from the place of the attack, the party divided, three tracks leading in a direction direct to Camp Date Creek; four toward the Hassayampa."

In all Captain Meinhold mentions seven tracks in his report. He chose to follow those seven tracks because of the exceptionally large size of one very distinctive track. He reported, "At a distance of about three miles both tracks joined, pointing toward the Hassayampa. I took measure in starting of one unusually large track, re-noticed it five or six times on the trail, and followed the seven plain and distinct tracks for a distance of twenty-two miles until near the Hassayampa Cañon." Later testimony provided by an Indian boy living with Dan O'Leary, an Arizona pioneer known for adopting orphaned Indians and raising them as his own, revealed that a small group of Indians divided from the main body of attackers and went to the O'Leary ranch, which was located at Walnut Creek north of Camp Date Creek and northwest of Prescott.

A pursuit posse was formed in Wickenburg at about midnight on November 5. The posse rode west on the La Paz Road to the site of the attack and took up the chase at first light. Following the erroneous report of the massacre in the November 11 edition of the *Miner*, members of the posse sent a letter to the editor. The "Corrected Account of the Massacre" was published on November 18 in the *Miner*. All members of the posse subscribed to the following account:

> So soon in the morning as it became light enough to see footprint, a party of our citizens were on the spot and took the trail. Judging from the indications after killing the passengers, something scared the Indians, causing them to leave in hot haste—scattering in different directions. After following up those different trails a distance of four or five miles they all united, forming one large trail, and heading towards the Date Creek Reservation. The trail showed them to be a party of Indians, some forty or fifty in number.

Captain Meinhold reported, "On the morning of the eighth I started out along the base of the range of mountains bordering the Date Creek–Wickenburg road in hopes to find the trail of the party in starting for the place where they lay in waiting for the stage. I did not strike it." Meinhold's lack of success in cutting the trail does not conclude that there was not a trail leading toward or away from the reservation. It was the military's inability to find and follow the tracks of Indians on foot that led to the employment of Indians as scouts.

There were reports that a sizeable number of Indians were absent from the Date Creek Reservation during the time of the massacre. The *Daily Alta California* reported, "The accounts received from Camp Date Creek state that during the 4th and 5th instants large numbers of the Reservation Indians were absent and did not return until the 6th." Captain Meinhold should have cut the trail of these Indians leaving the reservation. Later, those who would refute the allegations that Indians were responsible for the massacre would use the lack of an Indian trail to Camp Date Creek to prove that non-Indians were the guilty parties. This contention, however, does not withstand scrutiny when you consider that Mexicans or Whites would have left a much more visible trail, and this would have been apparent to Captain Meinhold during his scout of the region.

REMOVING/DESTROYING EVIDENCE

By 1871 the Indians were becoming adept at shifting blame, or at least trying to avoid blame, for their depredations. There was an incident at the Hugh's Ranch a few months previous to the massacre where Indians collected their arrows so that they could avoid detection. However, they missed one arrow in the soft earth of a newly plowed field. The markings on that arrow were used to identify the guilty parties.

Firearms recovered from Indians during the 1860s and early 1870s were ornately decorated, but, remarkably, the serial numbers were roughly defaced or gouged out to disguise their original owner. Indians knew that white and Mexican settlers could identify their personal firearms and other property, so during raids the Indians either left such property behind or disguised it.

Resulting from his investigation General Crook identified Chief Ocho-cama[22] as the leader of the stagecoach attack. Ocho-cama knew that he and his sub-chiefs had been identified as the ringleaders and believed that punitive action would soon follow. On September 8, 1872, Chief Ocho-cama led a group of fifty Indians to meet with General Crook at which time the chief conspired to kill Crook. After the chief was arrested, he escaped from the Date Creek guardhouse. The *Miner* reported that "according to his own confession, he murdered Mr. Leihy and Mr. Evarts in Hell's Canyon on November 10, 1866, for no other reason, he said, than that some person told him that Leihy had stolen some of his annuity goods. . . . His murderers tried to lay the blame of the crime on the Pimas, just as they have been in the habit of trying to make the Tontos shoulder their other evil deeds." Chief Ocho-cama was adept at avoiding guilt for his crimes.

CARDS WITH CORNERS CUT

Captain Meinhold reported, "On the left side and at a distance of 20–30 paces from the road . . . I found . . . a pack of Spanish cards, rounded at the corners in a manner I have seen cards in the hands of Indians at the Post." These playing cards were identified as the type used by the Apache-Mojave Indians for gambling. It is unlikely that Mexicans or Whites would have used them to squander the night hours while they awaited arrival of the stagecoach. However, Indian gaming cards of this description could have been easily obtained by Whites or Mexicans and planted at the scene. As such this item of evidence serves little purpose in determining the culprits.

BUTTER TINS AS CANTEENS

Captain Meinhold reported that near the place where he found the playing cards he also found "two tin cans (butter cans apparently) thrown away at some military post, picked up and used by the attacking parties to carry water." Butter tins were a popular medium among the Indians for carrying water. They preferred to obtain them full, so that they could make a small hole in the side and remove the contents by heating the container to the melting point and then draining the liquefied butter. Cans that had previously been opened were closed by tightly lacing a piece of hide over the opening. A small plug of wood or mescal stalk was then whittled and used to plug the side hole.

The makeshift canteens that Captain Meinhold found were determined to have been used to carry water to the ambush site. Mexicans or Whites would have used canteens or a water barrel, but they could have planted the butter tins at the scene to implicate Indians. The butter tins serve little purpose in identifying the culprits except that they add to the totality of the evidence.

DEFECATION

Captain Meinhold reported, "On the right side of the road, and a short distance from the place where the three or four had lain in ambush I found the places where some of the party had defacated [sic]. The excrements consisted of indigested [sic] melon seeds and mesquite beans." Several members of the attacking party excreted near the site of the attack during the time they awaited arrival of the stage. The excrement was closely examined at the scene by a skilled army officer who determined its nature and content.

Would Mexicans or Whites have eaten seeds and mesquite beans, planning to excrete evidence at the site? Drawing from his grandfather's memoirs, Dan Genung, in *Death in His Saddlebags*, wrote, "[The Yavapai] survived on mesquite beans, from which they made bread and a palatable drink. Charley [Genung—Dan's grandfather] knew from experience that mesquite beans caused stomach cramps in men and horses, but the hardy redmen suffered no such complaint."

More than six years after the massacre, the *Arizona Sentinel* reported, "An observant man soaked some of the dry excrement, washed the husks carefully, examined them and found them to be those of pumpkin seeds. Around Wickenburg Mexicans do not eat as many mezquite [*sic*] beans as Indians did, but they ate many times more pumpkin seeds." The article concludes that the presence of pumpkin seeds was evidence that the attackers were Mexicans. However, the attack was in November, well past the season for most melons but in the midst of the prime season for pumpkins. According to Genung, Mexicans did not eat Mesquite beans at all.

No conclusion can be drawn from the facts provided in the *Sentinel* article, if such an experiment was ever actually conducted. Indian excrement would undoubtedly have contained the seeds of whichever fruit or vegetable the Indians had recently raised or stolen. However, the presence of mesquite beans, if Charles Genung is correct, is clear evidence that the excrement came from Indians.

Following is the full text of that *Arizona Sentinel* article published on Saturday, August 3, 1878:

The Wickenburg, Arizona Massacre
Its True Story

At the time of its occurrence it was sought to attribute this massacre to Indians. The effect of doing this was thought to be to check a humanitarian feeling toward Indians that was fast growing up in the Eastern States and to give Arizona more troops and a larger money expenditure for army purposes. Army officers, contractors, and all citizens who professed to have at heart the welfare of this Territory, joined in preventing publication or even discussion, of such facts as tended to show that Indians had nothing whatever to do with it. But there were then men who arrived early at the scene of the tragedy, observant and qualified to draw correct conclusions, which thought then, and still think, that the murder and robbery were planned and committed by Americans and Mexicans.

The passengers were young Loring, *Tribune* correspondent, and a large, stout man, whose name we have lost, both just from Lieut. Wheeler's expedition; Salmon, also a topographical man on the same expedition; Shoholm, a jeweler of Prescott; C. S. Adams, clerk for Birchard and Co.; Kruger, Clerk of the Chief Quartermaster of the Department of Arizona; and Mollie Sheppard, who was reputed to have amassed much money as a courtezan at Prescott. The coming of the two latter had been freely talked about at Wickenburg, and it was generally believed that Kruger would bring thirty or forty thousand dollars of military funds, and that the woman would have at least fifteen thousand besides jewelry.

When the stage left Wickenburg about 9 a.m., Adams and Loring were on the outside; Salmon, Kruger and Mollie were inside on the back seat; Shoholm and the big man were on the front seat. It was November 5, 1871, and the weather being cold the curtains were all down. The inside passengers had spread a shawl on their laps and were playing freeze-out for a silver watch. When going up a wash, about seven miles westerly from Wickenburg, the stage was attacked from the right, or north side. Adams and Loring were shot off and fell into the road. John Lance, the driver, was shot through one arm, which dropped one string of reins and caused the team to swing into a gulch and clear around into the wash again, facing back toward Wickenburg. Meanwhile Lance had fallen off, dead from other wounds, Shoholm and the big man were shot in the back through the front of the stage and were found dead, fallen forward into the middle part of it. Salmon jumped out and ran about fifty yards, but was pursued and killed. Kruger and Mollie jumped out next to the bank of the gulch and, apparently, not realizing that the stage was turned around, ran behind it and continued running west and away from Wickenburg; this saved their lives. The position of the stage, the smoke and the inequalities of the ground concealed their flight, while pursuit of Salmon absorbed the attention of the murderers. Kruger was wounded slightly when the stage was fired into, and Mollie was accidentally shot through the left forearm while getting out. The wagon was completely riddled with bullet-holes. The two refugees walked about five miles, until about 3 p.m., they met the eastward-bound mail wagon, which was without passengers. Nelsen, the driver, gave them water, tied his team to the wagon, left them with it, and, mounting a saddle horse he was leading behind the wagon, rode to the Vulture Mine. There he told the story, got company, and reached the Wickenburg stage office at about 9 p.m. with the first news of the murder. A crowd was at once raised of horsemen and armed men and wagons sent out. Adams and Loring were found by the road; John Lance further on; Shoholm and the big man in the stage; Salmon was found the next day. No baggage had been opened except that of Kruger and Mollie Sheppard, which was marked with their names.

The mail bags had been cut; the letters were opened by having their ends torn off and were strewn by the road. No clothing had been carried off, nor had blankets, parti-colored rugs nor gay shawls; these were untouched. The weapons were all carried off except one pistol which was found under the driver's cushion, but ammunition was left in the wagon. No harness was cut nor was any strap or leather carried off. The off leader was dead, shot through the shoulder; the other three horses were unharnessed and turned loose with their collars on, and afterward recovered; one of them was found near Wickenburg that night, and drew stage over the same road for a long time afterward. The harnesses were found taken off and stacked up on the lead-bars and double-tresses just as if it had been done by some old hostler. The bodies were brought into Wickenburg and buried. The baggage was turned over to a Justice, but was all claimed by and delivered to Colonel O'Byrne [sic], commanding Camp Date Creek. Kruger and Mollie were also taken to Date Creek for care and treatment. It was afterwards stated that property from the massacre was found in the possession of some of the peace-professing Indians at Date Creek; but this statement was never verified. The only articles ever identified were some pieces of jewelry given to a Mexican woman by a man who was soon after killed at Phoenix.

The tracks of the attacking party were all made by moccasins. Mollie declared she caught sight of nine men, all clad in army overcoats, but that she could not tell whether they were Indians or not. Kruger used to tell about how they pursued him up the wash, and how he kept them at bay by presenting his pistol with one hand while he supported Mollie's fainting form with the other arm. Kruger says they were Indians, that he saw them. They certainly did not see him, for the perpetrators of such awful crime would not have let escape them an unarmed woman and a young man armed with only one pistol. Indians would have killed them at long rifle range, for fun. Whites would have done it for their own safety. No tracks had followed theirs up the wash.

The husks of mesquite [sic] beans were found in excrement of some of the murderers. This fact was dwelt upon as proof that Indians had committed the crime. An observant man soaked some of the dry excrement, washed the husks carefully, examined them and found them to be those of pumpkin seeds. Around Wickenburg Mexicans do not eat as many mezquite [sic] beans as Indians did, but they ate many times more pumpkin seeds.

Corroborating circumstantial evidence can be adduced by the bushel: conversations, remarks, etc., made before and after the occurrence. But the foregoing facts were all proven by the position of the bodies, stage, horses, tracks, etc.: and they are enough to convince any reflecting man acquainted with the Indian's passion for horse-meat, leather, clothing, and ammunition that the Wickenburg massacre was perpetrated by one or more Americans assisted by Mexicans.

In response to the *Sentinel* article the *Arizona Enterprise* wrote, on August 10, 1878:

The Yuma Sentinel believes in the old, old story concerning the Wickenburg massacre; thinks the bloody murders and heartless robberies were committed by whites and Mexicans. The Sentinel may know all about it. If so, its editor will please recollect the saying, "An open confession is good for the soul." Tell what you know, George, if you know anything. We have always contended in favor of the Indians and so did George Monroe and other citizens, who took care of the bodies and prospected with a view to determining the color of the fiends' faces who disgraced humanity by so brutal a massacre of innocent, unsuspecting people. General

Crook took great pains to find out the authors. His observations, etc., led him to believe that the devils were red ones. We have written whole columns, aye pages on the matter, but are ready to write some more whenever more light shall be thrown on the subject.

PROPERTY LEFT AT THE SCENE

Property left at the scene has been cited as proof-positive evidence by those professing that Whites or Mexicans attacked the stagecoach. The *Arizona Sentinel* of August 3, 1878, summarized that position: "But the foregoing facts were all proven by the position of the bodies, stage, horses, tracks, etc; and they are enough to convince any reflecting man acquainted with the Indian's passion for horse meat, leather, clothing and ammunition that the Wickenburg massacre was perpetrated by one or more Americans assisted by Mexicans."

Property left at the scene, suggesting non-Indian attackers, included:

Three live horses, which suggested non-Indian attackers. It was well known that Indians preferred horse meat over the meat of cattle or sheep. The Indians at Date Creek were starving so they would not have left three live horses at the scene. Mexicans or whites, knowing that the stock could be identified, would have.

The harness, which was stacked neatly upon the crossbars and doubletrees "as if by an old hostler." It was suggested that the Indians would have taken the leather, or at least they would not have stacked it as found. But wouldn't non-Indians, bent upon laying blame on Indians, have taken it if the Indians' passion for leather was so well known?

Curtains, colorful shawls, and most of the jewelry was left at the scene of the attack.

Pistol ammunition was left. A few sources suggest that several pistols were also left behind, but the pistol under the driver's seat was definitely not taken.

Despite this evidence, there was also property left at the scene that strongly suggests the perpetrators were Indians. This evidence included:

> two mailbags . . . though only one mail bag was cut and the only letters opened were addressed to "AQM" (Assistant Quarter Master) and "ACS" (Acting Commissary of Subsistence). These letters were opened carefully at one end and the contents were left inside the envelope. There is no explanation for Mexican or white perpetrators leaving one mailbag unopened, the other only selectively violated. They would have thoroughly searched both. Those letters opened would have contained only information. If just one of the Indians could read English, the disposition of the mail can be explained. An Indian identified by General Crook as one of the perpetrators—Chimhueva Jim—spoke and read English. The Indians, wards of the Government, would have been quite interested in any correspondence affecting their living conditions, materials, supplies, and continuing relationship with the army. Only the naivety or ignorance might explain the replacement of the contents, presumably believing that by doing so the violation of the letters would go unnoticed.

Money was left at the scene including a roll of greenbacks in plain sight on the ground near the stagecoach, and the Wells Fargo box was untouched in the driver's boot. Indians might have overlooked the greenbacks and the strong box. Would whites or Mexicans have been so careless as to leave the strong box when their intent was to intercept a gold shipment?

Only one passenger had been searched by the perpetrators. Charles Adams's pockets were found turned out. William George Salmon had eighty-four dollars in gold coin in his pockets. The murdered men had jewelry that was left on their bodies, though it was alleged in some literature that two watches and one watch fob were stolen. Mexican or white robbers most certainly would have been thorough in searching the bodies for valuables.

Most of the baggage was not searched. As a consequence many valuables were left behind. Indians were more likely to have left baggage unsearched, and especially if they found something to occupy their attention—such as the missing demi-john containing whiskey, six bottles of Jamaican Rum, and several bottles of porter. Whites or Mexicans would have been thorough in their search for valuables, but would probably not have taken the alcohol.

Some Apache-Mojave Indians, later identified by General Crook as being among the guilty, went to the Colorado River Indian Reservation where they boasted of their deeds to the Indians residing there. This information was shared with the agent at that reservation. On September 14, 1872, the *Miner* printed the following testimony collected by General Crook: "The murderers have said . . . they took very little clothing, trinkets, etc., fearing that the possession thereof might one day lead to their detection."

BRUSHY COVER CONSTRUCTED AT THE SCENE

In 1923 James H. Cook, recounting his fifty years on the frontier, wrote that the Indians "were, as a rule, poor shots with firearms.

Most of the white persons killed by them were fired upon at short range, from cover."

The men who attacked the Wickenburg-to-Ehrenberg stage-coach selected a poor site for their ambush, but enhanced it with makeshift cover. The *Miner*, on November 18, 1871, reported of the attackers: "They were secreted by the roadside behind piles of grass and shrubbery which they had collected and arranged in a manner that must fail to attract attention—by placing in an upright position, which gave them the appearance of clumps of shrubbery produced by the natural process of growth."

On November 21 the *Daily Alta California* reported that the attackers were positioned "at a distance of not over six feet from the stage." This was very short range for an attack with long arms.

Regarding the terrain, Captain Meinhold reported, "On the left side and at a distance of 20–30 paces from the road on an eminence which commands the view for a long distance of the road from Wickenburg." The reason that the small rise commanded such a view was that, except for a small canyon that divided two small foothills less than a mile south of the site, in every other direction the land was a flat, high mesa extending for many miles. Mexicans or Whites would have been more likely to have chosen a place with a blind turn or depression that blocked the roadway. Indians would have relied upon stealth, cunning, camouflage, surprise, and superior numbers rather than the terrain.

BUCKSKIN BAG CONTAINING BONE POWDER

Perhaps the most damning bit of evidence was an Apache-Mojave hunting bag containing bone powder that was found alongside the trail of moccasin tracks leading toward Camp Date Creek. In the "Corrected Account of the Massacre," the pursuit posse stated: "leaving on their trail many Indian articles (among others, bone dust used by the Indians as a medicine), which were brought in by Geo. Monroe."

Bone powder was sacred medicine to the Yavapai Indians and would not be given or sold to a Mexican or a white man. It would have been closely protected by its Indian owner and nearly impossible to steal. Its presence at the massacre site proves that there was at least one Apache-Mojave Indian in the ambush party. After examining this bag and its contents, Capt. John Bourke,[23] distinguished Indian ethnologist and author, became firmly convinced that the Date Creek Indians had attacked the Wickenburg stagecoach.

WATCH FOB

Much effort has been invested in attributing a silver watch fob found at the site of the attack to Frederick Loring. It was believed to have belonged to Loring because it displayed the initial "L."

The fob in question later passed into the possession of a woman from Wickenburg. That woman, characterized as a "soiled dove," claimed that she obtained the fob as a gift from Ramon Cordova.

Later Pvt. Berton "Lou" Shipp possessed the fob and brought the evidence to the attention of General Crook prior to his council with the Date Creek Indians on September 8, 1872. Private Shipp believed until his death that the fob belonged to Loring and that it was proof positive that Mexicans were responsible for the massacre. Private Shipp died in 1915 and the following article appeared in the *Miner* on May 16, 1916:

Frightful Deed of Early Days Recalled
Old Soldier Gives up
Relic Taken from One
of the Victims of
Wickenburg Massacre

Passing away on November 26 last, Berton L. Shipp left a request that relics which he had carried since 1872, be forwarded to the family of a man named Loring, a victim of the frightful Wickenburg Indian massacre of that year.

The property consisted of a watch fob made of silver, bearing the single letter "L." The address given was Somerville, Mass., with a message from the dying man of how and where it came into his possession.

Mr. Shipp stated that he had secured the emblem from a Mexican woman of Wickenburg about three months after the massacre occurred. At that time he was with a detachment of cavalry, out of Camp Date Creek, scouring the country for Apache Indians. Mr. Shipp was an enlisted soldier and gave as his reason for cherishing the silver piece that it served to identify him by his name, which was more familiarly known to comrades as "Lou." The newspaper account closes with the following statement made by Mr. Shipp: "From that day to the present time I will never believe the Indian had a hand in the Wickenburg massacre, and when on duty with my command, to ranking officers, including General George Crook, I showed them the silver piece, and told them how it came into my hands, as a bit of circumstantial evidence to base that belief. The woman who sold me the piece soon left for Southern Arizona and further investigation of from what source she received it could not be made. The following year my troop was ordered to Fort Apache, where I was mustered out, returning to San Jose, Cal. I have carried the mute evidence of a horrible crime committed in Arizona in the long ago and during these 44 years it has never been out of my possession a single minute. I trust there are some members of the family who survive, and that they will not treat my action in retaining the sad emblem, too harshly."

With all due respect to the late Mr. Shipp, there was never any evidence that Loring owned a watch or a fob. Photos of Loring taken only days before the massacre do not reveal a watch, but Loring's clothing was such that it could have concealed a watch from view.

The Loring family seemed surprised when contacted regarding the existence of the fob. They had made no effort to locate it previously when it was not returned among his effects. When they failed to receive it, they made no effort to confirm its continued existence or determine its whereabouts, which suggests they did not believe it belonged to Fred Loring.

If, by chance, Loring did own a fob and it was stolen during the massacre it could have come into the hands of Indians or the possession of Ramon Cordova by various means. Many of the Indians identified as guilty by General Crook went to the Colorado River Indian Reservation to dispose of their loot, including greenbacks and various trinkets. It is possible in this scenario that Ramon Cordova acquired the fob there, or he acquired it from someone who obtained it at that reservation and later sold it or gave it to him.

The fob serves little purpose in determining the guilty parties since it was never established whether or not it belonged to Loring or established how Cordova acquired it. The investigation was never pursued because the "soiled dove" reportedly moved to southern Arizona. However, all of Arizona was within the jurisdiction of General Crook, a man known to be diligent and tenacious in gathering information and evidence. Could it have been that the general already knew all the pertinent circumstances surrounding the fob before it came into the possession of Private Shipp?

GLOVE

Further evidence to prove the Indians guilty was provided by the evidence of a glove. The *Miner* carried the following article in its November 23, 1871, edition: "A report which we have not traced to its origin, but which is generally credited, says that a glove which has been recognized as having belonged to one of the victims of the Wickenburg murder, was found last week upon the person of an Indian at Camp Date Creek."

SHOT POUCH

Prescott's *Miner* reported in its November 9, 1872, edition that a shot pouch was found among the possessions of the Indians killed during the Burro Creek incident. Burro Creek is located at Muchos Cañons, and is the place where the remaining guilty Indians, those not captured or killed at the September 8 attack on General Crook, were surrounded and punished on September 25, 1872. The article stated: "More proof that it was Apache-Mohaves that murdered Loring, Hamel and other citizens, has come to light by the capture of a shot-pouch, bearing Hamel's name, in the recent fight with the murderers. This pouch, we learn, is now in possession of one of the men belonging to the pack train."

A shot pouch might be an item an Indian would retain for his own use and it would be an item that would have little value for sale or barter. It is difficult to see how an Indian would have come into possession of the particular shot pouch in question except by obtaining it from the scene of the attack or from another Indian who was there.

SCALPING

One controversy that has persisted is regarding which victims were scalped. It was reported, and still is the official opinion of the army, that William George Salmon was the only victim scalped.

Salmon strayed fifty to sixty yards eastward from the stagecoach during the attack. His body was not found by the rescue party during the early morning hours of November 6. He was, however, found the following morning sometime shortly after civil twilight by the pursuit posse. He was buried in a deep grave near the roadway so that the pursuit posse could continue on the trail of the attackers. The pursuit posse reported to Captain Meinhold that Salmon had been scalped "chin to nape," a manner characteristic of Apache-Mojave Indians.

On November 21 the *Daily Alta California* published a communication received from Wickenburg dated November 8: "Mr. Salmon received a severe wound and fell from the stage, but recovering ran about twenty yards, was followed, overtaken, killed and scalped, the whole hair, ears, skin of the face being taken off to the mouth."

However, despite this evidence, at the inquest it was reported that P. M. Hamel was scalped in the Apache-Mojave manner—top knot only and discarded at the site of the scalping ritual. In yet another account, Charles Genung reported that it was Charles Adams who was the one scalped.

The *Miner*, on November 18, summarized the scalping ritual: "And those who are best acquainted with the Indian customs believe that he [Hamel] must have fought bravely for his life as he was the only member of the party who was scalped—it being customary with the savages to disfigure the bodies of those who fall while fighting to defend their lives."

So who was scalped? Actually, the evidence supports the conclusion that both Salmon and Hamel were scalped. The inquest jury's verdict stated: "We the undersigned . . . do find . . . P. M. Hamel [the one found scalped] . . ." The nine-man jury could hardly have been mistaken about the scalping of Hamel, as Hamel's fresh body was laid before them for careful examination.

Capt. Charles Meinhold did not arrive in Wickenburg until Monday evening—nearly thirty-six hours after the attack, after the inquest, and after the bodies were buried in the private graveyard of Henry Wickenburg. There is no indication or mention in his report that he viewed the body of Hamel or any of the other victims' bodies, or that he felt any responsibility to do so. Perhaps he declined to investigate or report upon the condition of the remains because the bodies were in the hands of civil authorities. George Monroe of the pursuit posse, one of those who found and buried Salmon, did not see Hamel's remains either.

However, it was Captain Meinhold's duty to investigate the scene of the attack and that included the grave site of Salmon. Captain Meinhold either exhumed the body for examination or took Monroe's word for the scalping of Salmon. The Captain reported: "On the left side of the road, about sixty yards back towards Wickenburg, is the grave of Mr. Salmon, who mortally wounded, got out of the coach and was killed and scalped (the only one scalped) by the attacking party on the spot where he was buried."

It is likely that George Monroe and the members of the inquest jury could not have been mistaken about a matter so apparent, and each party had sufficient time to make a careful examination of the body which, by circumstances, had been placed in their care. One can only conclude that both men were scalped, but that no member of either group reporting their observations had occasion to see both bodies.

Was there anyone who knew of both scalpings? William Kruger had apparently heard and accepted the reports of both the inquest jury and the pursuit posse. He could not have seen Salmon's body when he "stopped at the place of the attack and closed the eyes of all my poor traveling companions," because had he found Salmon's body at that time it would have been returned to Wickenburg with the others.

It was the second party, the pursuit posse, which found and buried Salmon's remains in a deep cut in the side of a hill. In his letter to William G. Peckham dated December 9, 1871, Kruger states: "The latter one [Salmon] was mortally wounded and fell out of the stage, and crawled away, but was finally captured by the Indians, scalped and otherwise mutilated . . . The other man who got scalped was buried on the road." The "other man" was Salmon, Hamel being the first man he knew to be scalped.

Finally, as to the report by Charles Genung regarding the scalping of Charles S. Adams, the body of Adams lay before the inquest jury with ample time for a careful examination. The jury failed to comment on his scalping but rather commented that Hamel was the only one found scalped. If Adams had been scalped it would have been quite obvious to every juror. Therefore, one must conclude that Adams was not scalped and that Charles Genung's report can be dismissed as error or faulty memory.

THE BODIES

The bodies of the massacre victims were buried following the inquest on Monday, November 6, 1871. The burial took place before the arrival of Captain Meinhold on the evening of the same date. The *Daily Alta California* reported, "The dead were buried the next day, Church services read over them." While the nights were cool in early November 1871, the days were warm and the bodies would not have kept well, especially considering the condition of open wounds exuding bodily fluids as well as the normal functional evacuations resulting from sudden, violent death. Burial would have been justifiably expedited.

In his report Captain Meinhold did not mention the bodies of the five victims that were the subject of the inquest or comment on their condition. That implies that he did not see the bodies. Had he seen them he surely would have commented and that would have resolved the controversy over who was scalped.

The bodies of five victims, which were immediately taken to Wickenburg, were interred side by side in the southeast corner of the private graveyard set aside by Henry Wickenburg. Kruger, in a letter to William G. Peckham, stated: "Loring and four of his companions in fate were decently buried the next day, Monday, November 6th, 1871, in nice coffins. I saw them buried." It was Mr. John Sexton, proprietor of the Vulture Mine and a prominent Wickenburg resident, who saw to the burial and provided five coffins.

Henry Wickenburg's private graveyard still exists, but the graves were disturbed in October 1949. Thereafter, the disposition of the remains of the massacre's dead is unknown.

The body of the sixth victim, William George Salmon, was moved to Wickenburg several months after the massacre. Under the headline Colyer's Human Plantation, the January 27, 1872, edition of the *Miner* reported: "The remains of Geo. Salmon, one of the victims of the Wickenburg massacre, was last week removed from the place of burial—at the scene of the slaughter—and placed beside those of his fellow travelers who fell with him. This humane and benevolent act was done at the insistence of Mr. James Grant, mail contractor, and under the direction of Dr. J. Pierson. The bodies of the six murdered men now rest side by side, at Wickenburg."

A letter to Lt. George M. Wheeler on March 15, 1872, confirms the reinterment. Capt. Richard F. O'Bierne, commanding the post at Camp Date Creek, wrote, "The remains of Mr. Salmon have been decently buried by the side of the others who were killed at the same time."

Kruger's letter to William G. Peckham, written soon after the massacre, provides important information about the event. It was published in the *Army and Navy Journal* on Saturday, January 6, 1872. The entire text follows:

The Army and Navy Journal
Volume IX, Number 21
Twenty-first Infantry

From Boston a correspondent of the *New York Times* sends the following letter from one of the survivors of the Loring massacre, giving an account of that massacre, and reflecting on the conduct of one of the officers of this regiment with reference to it. We publish the letter as it bears a responsible signature, but shall be glad to publish any correction of its statements:

Ehrenberg, A.T., December 9th, 1871
William G. Peckham, Esq.
Trinity Building, New York

Dear Sir:

In acknowledging the receipt of your letter of November 16th, 1871, I am pleased to be able to give you an account of the death of my friend Loring, who was well known to me and whose untimely death is deeply regretted by me. We left Fort Whipple, near Prescott, Arizona Territory, on Saturday, November 4th, in the best of health and spirits. To be sure, the stage was rather crowded, but being all of such good temper we had a real nice time, Loring being the most lively of us all, anticipating a speedy return to his friends East. Well, he retained his inside seat until we reached Wickenburg, on Sunday morning, November 5th, 1871, when, after leaving there, he preferred to have an outside seat, to which I most decidedly objected; but he insisted on being outside for a short time. I had two revolvers and he had none; in fact, no arms whatever. He rejected my offer of a revolver, saying at the same time, "My dear Kruger, we are now comparatively safe. I have traveled with Lieutenant Wheeler for nearly eight months, and have never seen an Indian." Well, we rolled on until about 11 a.m., when the fatal attack was made. The first warning I had was the warning of the driver, who cried "Apaches! Apaches!" At the same moment the Indians, who lay concealed, fired the first volley, killing poor Loring, the driver, and the other outside passenger, a Mr. Adams. They killed also the off lead horse and wounded the other lead horse. The horses very much frightened, then ran forward about twenty yards, when they came to a sudden stop. At the same time Loring fell off the stage and so did the other passenger. At the same moment the Indians fired the second volley from three sides—the both sides and rear—not more than four or five yards from the stage, killing Mr. Shoholm, one of the inside passengers, and wounding Ms. Sheppard, myself and a Mr. Salmon, of Lieutenant Wheeler's party. The latter one was mortally wounded and fell out of the stage, and crawled away, but was finally captured by the Indians, scalped and otherwise mutilated. The only one not then wounded was Mr. Hamel, of Lieutenant Wheeler's party. Both he and myself commenced immediately firing. Each one fired six shots. Not having any more ammunition I ceased firing. The Indians then disappeared behind the bushes.

But what a terrible spectacle it was to see the six dead bodies in plain sight! Loring was lying right under my very eyes, not yet dead but suffering, apparently, terribly. He was shot through his left temple, his right eye, and his lungs. He suffered for about four minutes, but I am positive that he died before I made my escape. Knowing that it would be useless to attempt to escape until the Indians would come back to plunder the stage, I remained perfectly quiet, having in the mean time ascertained that Ms. Sheppard was yet alive, but badly wounded. She succeeded in getting a loaded revolver from one of the killed passengers, which she gave to me. I then told her to keep cool and be ready to run as soon as I would give the signal. Well, in about six minutes of terrible suspense I saw the Indians slowly creeping toward the stage. I counted and saw plainly fifteen Indians all dressed in blue soldiers' trousers. When they came within five yards of the stage I jumped up, yelled and fired at them. The woman, at the same time, yelled also, and we succeeded admirably in driving them off for the time being, and got time to leave the stage. Before I left the stage I cried out as loud as I possibly could if anyone was left alive, but only Mr. Adams answered; but he was mortally wounded and could not even move his hands or feet, so I had to leave him to his fate. He was afterward found with his throat cut and otherwise mutilated. The Indians afterward followed me for about five miles, and I had a running fight with them until I fell in with the "buck-board." I had to carry the wounded woman for over two miles in my left arm. I myself received one shot through the right armpit, coming out on the shoulder, and two shots in my back. The woman also had three shots, one dangerous.

How I could escape with my life, and be able to save the life of Ms. Sheppard, is more than I can account for. That I left my mark with the Indians, there is no doubt, because two Indians died from gun-shot wounds at Camp Date Creek Reservation; but the commanding officer refused to have the thing investigated for fear he would find sufficient evidence that they were his pets, that is, Camp Date Creek Indians. At all events there is no doubt whatever that the outrage was committed by Indians, and that by Camp Date Creek Indians, those so-called friendly Indians whom Uncle Sam feeds.

After the news reached Wickenburg, we were brought to Wickenburg after sixteen hours of terrible suffering and agony. I stopped at the place of attack and closed the eyes of all my poor traveling companions. Loring, poor boy, was not mutilated, but looked calm and peaceful, excepting his fearful wounds through the head. He wore soldiers' clothing. His hat is in my possession now; if you wish it you can have it. Loring and four of his companions in fate were decently buried the next day, Monday, November 6th, 1871, in nice coffins. I saw them buried. The other man who got scalped was buried on the road. Mr. Sexton, of the Vulture Mill, at Wickenburg, attended to the funeral. Rest assured that our friend Loring had a decent funeral. Peace be with his ashes. I forwarded everything belonging to Loring to Lieutenant Wheeler, excepting his hat, which you can have should you desire it. There are four bullet-holes through the same. What Loring lost I don't profess to know. I know, I lost everything but my life. The Indians got, to my certain knowledge, about twenty-five thousand dollars—nine thousand dollars belonging to me and Ms. Sheppard.

There is not a particle of doubt in my mind that the attacking party were Indians. I have known Indians since the last five years and cannot be mistaken; besides, all indications show that they were Indians. Every citizen here will swear to it, because these citizens tracked the Indians from the place of outrage to Camp Date Creek. But the commanding officer, Captain O'Beirne, Twenty-first Infantry, not only allowed the Indians to go unpunished, but also refused me, Ms. Sheppard, the two surviving cripples, shelter. Yes sir; he ordered us off his reservation and I wish to heaven you would publish this act of inhumanity in your New York papers. Please show this letter to Mr. Loring, Boston, Mass., who wrote to me the same time you did.

I am sir,
Very truly yours,
William Kruger
Chief Clerk to Captain
C. W. Foster, Q. M.,
U.S.A.

In April of 1871, more than one hundred settlers slaughtered 135 Apaches (mostly old men, women, and children) at Camp Grant, along Arizona's Arivaipa Creek. The defendants, pictured here, were found not guilty of their crimes, a clear indication of the settlers' attitude toward Native Americans.

Captain George Hall Burton investigated reports that Indians from the Date Creek Reservation had bragged of their part in the Wickenburg massacre.

General George Crook faced several crisis during his years in Arizona but none more challenging than the Wickenburg massacre. He spent two years investigating the crime, taking no punitive action until he knew the name of each participant.

e scene of the Wickenburg massacre, facing south toward the hill from which the Indians made their attack.

The officers of the Third Cavalry were photographed in Montana several years after the Wickenburg massacre. They were led by Captain Charles Meinhold (1), First Lieutenant Joseph H. Lawson (2) and Second Lieutenant James F. Simpson (3). These three men were posted on the Date Creek Indian Reservation in November 1871, and each played a role in the initial investigation of the massacre. This is the only known photograph of Captain Meinhold.

The majority of the goods that supplied the day-to-day needs of Arizona's scattered community came to the area via California freighters.

*A graduate of Harvard University, Frederick Wadsworth Loring went
west as a journalist, attached to a surveying expedition. Eight miles
outside of Wickenburg, he met his end, a death that played a large
role in reversing public sympathy with the Indian tribes of the
Southwest. The Wickenburg massacre has sometimes been called
the "Loring massacre."*

A major player in the desert southwest, surveyor Lieutenant George Wheeler conducted fourteen expeditions between 1871 and 1879.

Charles Genung, a prominent Arizona pioneer, was biased against the region's Mexican population. He tried to shift the blame for the Wickenburg massacre from Indians to Mexicans.

Wells, Fargo & Company "express" boxes were made in San Francisco by J. Y. Ayers, who used ponderosa pine reinforced with oak rims and secured with iron straps. A box typically measured twenty inches long, twelve inches wide, and ten inches deep and weighed about twenty-five pounds "lean."

The Concord stagecoaches were built by a company in Concord, New Hampshire, and typically could carry up to twenty-one people, which means that the coach bound for Ehrenberg was nearly empty when it was attacked.

WERE WHITE MEN INVOLVED?

Mollie Sheppard, during her interview with Captain Meinhold on the evening of November 6, made a comment that prompted him to record the following in his official report: "The woman Sheppard is under the impression that white men were among the robbers, but she has no other reason to advance than that she had heard that certain parties in Prescott, who disappeared about the time she left Prescott, had made inquiries about the time of her departure and what amount of money she was likely to carry with her."

Ms. Sheppard's concern was provoked by second-hand information and can easily be explained by the fact that residents of Prescott were working men who would "disappear" from town to pursue work on a ranch or in a mine. Mollie Sheppard was a beautiful young woman, sought after, and quite successful in her chosen profession of prostitution. The inquiries about her trip could have been made by faithful clients, crestfallen over her leaving and concerned that she would have sufficient resources to sustain herself. Mollie Sheppard, though renowned for being close with a dollar, had been an angel of mercy to the poor and the sick of Prescott. As such, many of them may have been concerned over her leaving and might have asked regarding her situation.

In any case, there is not one item of evidence that any white man was involved in the massacre, though rumors and accusations proliferated. These accusations include the involvement of a man named Charles Stanton as either a backer, as being personally involved in the massacre, or as part of his work in the Indian Rings.

Ms. Sheppard's distrust of the upright citizens of Prescott could as easily have stemmed from her battle with the Yavapai County Board of Supervisors over the taxes she owed for her house. She had fought the board for nearly three years until they finally succeeded in driving her from Prescott.

All the subsequent conjecture about white involvement began with that one innocent statement by Ms. Sheppard—that she heard of white men asking about her. But then, they were always asking about her, so her claims couldn't be substantiated.

BLUE PANTS

It was reported by both survivors that the attackers wore the blue cavalry pants that were commonly given to Indians on reservations. Mexicans or Whites could have obtained the pants as well. However, judging from the ferocity of the assault, the attackers expected that everyone would be dead. Why would the attackers concern themselves with wearing army pants to disguise themselves as "Indian" if there were to be no witnesses? Since blue army pants would have been available to any group of attackers, they serve little purpose in identifying the murderers.

GAIT, APPEARANCE AND BEARING

William Kruger stated during his interview in Los Angeles on January 3, 1872, that the attackers "had the gait, appearance and bearing of the Apaches during the whole time they were under [our] observation, which it would have been impossible for any Whites or Mexicans to have assumed and maintained." His statement most certainly refers to their distinct way of walking toe-in. No one can disagree that it would be difficult for Whites or Mexicans to maintain "the gait, appearance, and bearing" of Indians for very long, and that they would naturally return to a walking demeanor normal for their race, especially when not under direct observation.

It can be assumed that the seven tracks followed by Captain Meinhold and company for over twenty-two miles, as well as the forty to fifty tracks followed by George Monroe's[24] posse, maintained the toe-in gait and appearance throughout the entire distance they were followed. If the footprints had been doctored, there would surely have been extensive reporting of that fact by all parties.

DENOMINATIONS OF GREENBACKS

Testimony provided by an Apache-Mojave Indian boy revealed that a small group of Indians went to the ranch of Dan O'Leary[25] with a large quantity of greenbacks. The boy was the adopted son of O'Leary. Dan Thrapp, in the book *Dan O'Leary, Arizona Scout; A Vignette,* noted, "On various occasions O'Leary was known to have raised some Indian waif, and to have done it with a kindliness that the youngsters never forgot." The Indians traveling to O'Leary's ranch were probably those responsible for the seven pairs of moccasin tracks followed by Captain Meinhold, tracks which pointed in the direction of the Hassayampa Cañon.

Therefore, it becomes critical in this investigation to locate O'Leary's ranch to explain the eastward direction of the tracks. Thrapp reported that in May 1869 "Dan . . . bought a place near Camp Tollgate, on Walnut Creek, in Yavapai County. Here O'Leary more or less settled for a few years." Camp Tollgate was located thirty-five miles northwest of Prescott at the tollgate of the Prescott–Fort Mojave Road. Camp Tollgate was renamed Camp Hualpai in 1870 and abandoned in 1873.

O'Leary was still living on Walnut Creek near Camp Hualpai on March 2, 1872, when a neighbor, Andy Stainbrook, mistook him for a deer in the brush and took a shot at him. The *Arizona Citizen* on June 22, 1872, reported, "He [O'Leary] has always lived somewhere from the Colorado River along up to Prescott, and is especially proud of the valley and the people about (Camp) Hualpai."

Indians had great difficulty discerning one denomination of greenback from another. Dan Genung, in *Death in His Saddlebags*, noted this difficulty among the Yavapai who worked for his grandfather and quotes from his grandfather's memoirs: "Once the money arrived, another difficulty arose because the Indians could not distinguish between five dollar and two dollar bills. The white men were constantly interrupted to tell the difference."

O'Leary's Indian boy reported to General Crook that seven Indians summoned him to explain the denominations of their greenbacks. The boy identified the Indians who had sent for him as members of the Apache-Mojave tribe living on the Date Creek Reservation.

INVESTIGATIVE REPORT OF CAPTAIN CHARLES MEINHOLD

Following is the full text of the report submitted to Lieutenant Ebstein, Date Creek Post Adjutant, by Capt. Charles Meinhold.

In obedience to Special Orders No. 120, G.S. Hqtrs. Camp Date Creek, I proceeded on the 6th inst. to the point on the La Paz road, where the mail stage was attacked on the morning of the 5th inst. to ascertain the particulars connected with the attack, and by what parties it was made.

I submit the following as the result of my investigation.

I arrived late on the evening of the 6th inst., at Wickenburg where I found, in the house of Mr. Sexton, proprietor of the Vulture Mine, Mr. Kreuger, Clerk of Captain

Foster, A.Q.M. Mr. Kreuger was slightly wounded. From him I learned that the following passengers were on board the stage:

1st   The driver (whose name has escaped my memory)
2nd Ms. Sheppard of Prescott
3rd   Mr. F. W. Loring }
4th   P. M. Hamel} employees of Lieutenant Wheeler
5th   G. S. Salmon}
6th   Mr. Adams, formerly agent of the firm of Birchard & Co.
7th   Mr. F. W. Shoholm of Prescott
8th   Mr. Kreuger

At a distance of about 8 miles from Wickenburg and at 8 o'clock a.m. on the 5th the stage was attacked by a party of Indians (10–12 in number). The party fired into the coach from both sides of the road, killing at the first fire one horse, and all the passengers but himself, Ms. Sheppard, and Mr. Salmon. The two former were slightly injured and Mr. Salmon, mortally wounded. Mr. Kreuger and Ms. Sheppard got out of the coach and ran, pursued by some of the Indians into the bushes on the left side of the road. The pursuit was however soon abandoned, and Mr. Kreuger and the wounded woman walked along the road toward Collins Ranch, until they met the Mail from Ehrenberg. The driver obtained assistance in Wickenburg, and Mr. Kreuger and the woman were brought in and taken care of.

Mr. Kreuger is positive in his assertions that the attacking party were Indians.

On the following morning I examined in person the spot where the attack was made; it is at a distance of about 8 miles from Wickenburg, at a point where the road turns down a little hill into a dry arroyo. On the right side of the road, and close to it, is a large mesquite bush under which I discovered three or four moccasin tracks of the pattern used by the Apache-Mojaves, on the left side and at a distance of 20–30 paces from the road on an eminence which commands the view for a long distance of the road from Wickenburg, I found as many more tracks of the same description, also two tin cans (butter cans apparently) thrown away at some Military Post, picked up and used by the attacking parties to carry water, a pack of Spanish cards rounded at the corners, in a manner I have seen cards in the hands of Indians at this Post. On the right side of the road, and a short distance from the place where three or four had lain in ambush I found the places where some of the party had defacated [sic]. The excrements consisted of undigested melon seeds and Mesquite beans. On the left side of the road, about sixty yards back towards Wickenburg, is the grave of Mr. Salmon, who mortally wounded got out of the coach and was killed and scalped (the only one scalped) by the attacking party on the spot where he was buried. I then proceeded to ascertain the direction the party had taken after the murder and robbery had been committed. About one half mile from the place of the attack the party divided, three tracks leading in a direction direct to Camp Date Creek, four toward the Hassayampa. At a distance of about three miles both tracks joined, pointing toward the Hassayampa. I took measure of one unusually large track, re-noticed it five or six times on the trail, and followed the seven plain and distinct tracks for a distance of twenty-two miles until near the Hassayampa Cañon so many tracks crossed, re-crossed, and followed the trail that I found it impossible to trace the seven tracks any longer.

On the morning of the eighth I started out along the base of the range of mountains bordering the Date Creek Wickenburg road in hopes to find the trail of the party in starting for the place where they lay in waiting for the stage. I did not strike it. I then crossed the mountains into Peeples Valley where I found many Indians quietly working for the settlers. Today I returned to the Post, crossing the mountain range known by the name of Date Creek Mountain.

I beg leave to add what I have heard in Wickenburg in regard to the attacking party whether it consisted of Indians or Mexicans, or white men. Some suspect the Mexican Rancheros of Hassayampa Cañon, others assert that such a scheme had been planned for some time, that it was intended to rob the mail of the bullion generally shipped on or shortly after the 1st of every month. Others, and I found them rather in a minority, accuse the Indians living at this Post. The woman Sheppard is under the impression that white men were amongst the robbers, but she has no other reason to advance than that she had heard that certain parties in Prescott, who disappeared suddenly about the time she left Prescott, had made inquiries about the time of her departure and what amount of money she was likely to carry with her.

I ascertained that no horses were stolen nor any baggage, that even the persons of the passengers were not searched and robbed except Mr. Adams whose pockets were found to be turned inside out. Mr. Adams is or has been the agent of Mr. Birchard and was likely to be thought carrying a large amount of money.

I also noticed that while many letters were not interfered with, almost every one addressed to an A. Q. M or A. C. S. was opened and that all the letters I saw opened had

been opened carefully at one end and the contents restored
in many cases.

> I am sir,
> Very Respectfully,
> Your Obed. Servant
> [Signed] Chas. Meinhold
> Captain, 3rd U.S. Cavalry

NEWSPAPER ACCOUNTS OF THE TRAGEDY

The newspaper report published immediately following the tragedy
in the *Miner* on November 11, 1871, provided the first account of
the tragedy. Although later accounts would clarify many minute
details, it is surprising to see how thorough and accurate newspaper
reporting was during those early days. It was also this first account
which was the source for a campaign by Charles Genung that later
led to the controversy about who was responsible.

The Wickenburg Horror
Murder and Robbery on the Highway.
Were they Indians or Mexicans?

The mail due at this place on Monday, arrived early in
the afternoon of Tuesday, bringing the particulars, so far as
known, of one of the bloodiest deeds ever committed in
Arizona. At an early hour on Sunday morning, the 5th inst.,
the mail stage on the route from Wickenburg to Ehrenberg
left the former place with the driver, John Lanz [sic], and the
following named passengers: Frederick Shoholm, Frederick
W. Loring, P. M. Hamel, W. G. Salmon, C. S. Adams, Wm.
Kruger and Ms. Sheppard. At a point about nine miles from
Wickenburg a party of mounted men—

Either Indians or Mexican Bandits

disguised after the fashion of Apache warriors—rushed down upon the stage as it was passing through a canyon and fired a volley into the passengers, killing all but two persons and slightly wounding these. The wounded—Mr. Kruger and Ms. Sheppard—not being disabled immediately sprang from the stage, which was now brought to a halt, and started together toward Culling's Station. While one detachment of the bloodthirsty demons surrounded the stage, the balance went in pursuit of the fugitives and kept up a desultory fire; but being all mounted, their aim was unsteady, so that beyond a slight wound received by Ms. Sheppard, neither sustained further injury than the wounds inflicted by the first fire. This pursuit was kept up for a distance of nearly half a mile—the pursuers being, meanwhile, kept at bay by Mr. Kruger who still retained his revolver, and fired upon them whenever they drew too near, causing them to scatter and retreat, but only to rally again to the pursuit until finally they withdrew and joined their fellows. The fugitives continued on their way toward Culling's Wells until they hailed the eastward bound mail, a few miles from that station. Here they were picked up by the driver who retraced his steps to the station, from which point information of the calamity was sent to Wickenburg via the Vulture mine; the bearer fearing to proceed by the direct route. The despatch reached Wickenburg about midnight when two parties of citizens

Started for the Scene

one to bring in the dead and the other, under command of Geo. Monroe, to take the trail of the murderers. Upon reaching the stage a most horrible picture was presented to their sight. Six men—Messrs. Loring, Shoholm, Lanz [sic], Hamel, Adams, and Salmon who, eighteen hours previous, left Wickenburg full of life and hope and in the happy anticipation of soon again greeting their friends after a prolonged absence—lay side by side, rigid in death and drenched in blood—the unavenged victims of a murder as dark and as damnable as ever stained the hands of an assassin.

The Mystery

which surrounds the identity of the murderers exists in the disposition which was made of the mail and baggage: one mail sack was cut open and its contents scattered over the ground, the other was left untouched. The baggage of the passengers was broken open, and while articles of but little value were carried away, large sums of money and other valuables remained. All this would suggest the work of ignorant savages; but, as neither the arms, ammunition nor animals had been removed, some are inclined to the opinion that the outrage was perpetrated by a band of Mexican bandits from Sonora. Mr. Kruger, who has really had the best opportunity of deciding this question, states positively that they were Indians. But, at all events, the next mail may bring reports which will place the guilt of this terrible crime where it properly belongs; when we hope it will not be left to the local authorities of Arizona to redress the wrong, or, rather, to avenge an outrage against this Government and people at large.

The Victims—Who Were They

Frederick W. Loring was twenty-two years of age and a native of Boston. He graduated from Harvard in 1870 and immediately engaged in the business of journalism in Boston. Early in the present year he joined the Wheeler Expedition which he accompanied throughout all its rambles, arriving here two weeks ago on his way home. Although a boy in years, Mr. Loring was a mature man in mind whose name had become familiar to almost every reader as an author and "contributor" of rare merit.

Messrs. Hamel and Salmon were likewise members of the Wheeler Expedition. Both gentlemen were residents of San Francisco where the latter leaves a wife and two small children who were entirely dependent upon his labor for support.

Mr. Shoholm was returning to his home in Philadelphia after an absence of many years, part of which time he was a member of the firm of Jewell & Co. of this town.

C. S. Adams leaves a wife and three small children in San Francisco. For the last ten months he had charge of the flour depot of W. Birchard & Co. at this place and was on his way to join his family in San Francisco.

The driver, John Lanz [sic], was recently from California, had obtained a situation as driver a few days before, and was making his first trip from Wickenburg.

The corrected account of the massacre published on November 18, 1871, provides additional information, especially regarding the findings of the pursuit posse. This article stated that the particulars of the first article were nearly complete, but affirmed the opinion that the attack was done by Indians. This article described the scene and presented a reasonable sequence of the events during the attack that led to six deaths.

A Corrected Account of the Massacre—The Inquest

Last week we gave an account of the capture of the mail stage and the murder of five passengers and the driver near Wickenburg. Our account was gathered from a series of conflicting verbal reports and although inaccurate in a few particulars was, in the main, correct. Subsequent mails have brought us the particulars of the outrage, which we now propose to place before our readers.

In the first place, then, there is no longer a doubt as to the authors of the crime. They were Indians—Apache-Mojaves—from the Date Creek Reservation. They were secreted by the roadside behind piles of grass and shrubbery which they had collected and arranged in a manner that must fail to attract attention—by placing in an upright position, which gave them the appearance of clumps of shrubbery produced by the natural process of growth. In the second instance the murderers were not mounted, but were all on foot. The hiding places which we have described extended for some distance along the roadside, and when the stage had reached a point about the middle of the line it was raked by the fire of the assassins in three directions—in front, in rear and directly opposite the sides. The driver and three of the passengers were killed outright at the first fire and the remaining four passengers, with one exception, wounded. At this time the survivors were Ms. Sheppard, and Messrs. Kruger, Hamel and Loring. The last-named had thus far escaped. As the Indians were rushing upon the stage after firing the first volley, Ms. Sheppard and Mr. Kruger sprang to the ground, at the side opposite to that from which they were approaching, and escaped with their lives. Unfortunately for Messrs. Loring and Hamel, in the excitement of the moment they lost all presence of mind and sprang from the stage at the side occupied by the Indians. The former being unarmed could offer no resistance and so endeavored to escape by flight. But the effort was hopeless; he was in the center of a group of savages and there fell, pierced by two bullets and dispatched by a lance thrust in the breast. Mr. Hamel was killed about the same instant; and those who are best acquainted with the Indian customs believe that he must have fought bravely for his life as he was the only member of the party who was scalped—it being customary with the savages to disfigure the bodies of those who fall while fighting to defend their lives.

At a late hour on Sunday night the victims were brought to Wickenburg and on the following day an inquest was held on the bodies.

The following is a copy of the verdict rendered:

We the undersigned—summoned as a jury to hold an inquest on the bodies of the following named persons found murdered in the stagecoach about six miles from the town of Wickenburg on the La Paz road on the morning of the 5th of November 1871—from all the evidence obtained from the two surviving passengers, do find that C. S. Adams, John Lent [sic], Fred W. Loring, Fred W. Shoholm, W. G. Salmon and P. M. Hamel (found scalped) came to their death by gunshot wounds received at the hands of Indians trailed towards the Date Creek Reservation.

> F. Purcella
> David Morgan
> Aaron Barnett
> Chas. H. Richardson
> Julius A. Goldwater
> M.W. Webber
> Dennis May
> Chas. Barbour
> Mack Morris, Foreman

In addition to the foregoing account, which we have received from persons who visited the scene of the massacre we append the following letter from Wickenburg, written under date of November 12th:

Editors Miner:

In looking over the last issue of your paper (Nov. llth) report giving details concerning the late tragedy which occurred near our place, I wish to correct one error; the murderers were not "mounted on horses," but all on foot and wearing the Apache moccasins, leaving on their trail many Indian articles (among others, bone dust used by the Indians as a medicine), which were brought in by Geo. Monroe.

The affair is a serious one and unprecedently bold, therefore our citizens wish to have the blame attached to none but the guilty ones, consequently they have spared no trouble nor expense thoroughly satisfying themselves. So soon in the morning as it became light enough to see a foot-print, a party of our citizens were on the spot and took the trail. Judging from the indication after killing the passengers, something scared the Indians causing them to leave in hot haste—scattering in different directions. After following up those different trails a distance of four or five miles they all united, forming one large trail and leading towards the Date Creek Reservation. The trail showing them to be a party of Indians, some forty or fifty in number, it was useless for the few citizens then on the trail to follow them further, the Indians having some twenty hours the start, so they returned to Wickenburg where they met Capt. Meinhold with a detachment of troops from Camp Date Creek with orders to use all efforts to find out who the murderers were. Thereupon Mr. Monroe and Mr. Frink immediately returned with Capt. Meinhold and his command, again took the trail and followed it until citizens and Soldiers were all thoroughly satisfied of the perpetrators of this horror.

We being the scouting party subscribe to the above being a true report: being the first on the ground, after the massacre, and of the last who left the trail.

> W. J. Barclay
> Geo. Monroe
> Edward Prentiss
> Geo. Bryan
> Jose M. Salallo

Chapter 5

Crook Goes for Them

For those who would divert blame away from the Apache-Mojave Indians and place it upon Whites or Mexicans, it became necessary to attack the messenger—Gen. George Crook. General Crook was a man of honesty and integrity in both his personal and professional life. His assignment to the Arizona Territory had been requested by Governor A. P. K. Safford, who wanted him to replace General Stoneman. Gen. Philip H. Sheridan finally assigned Crook to the Arizona Territory, over his protest, and Crook entered the territory in June 1871. General Crook, known by the Indians as "Nantan Lupan" or grey wolf, was respected by friends and enemies. He was never quick to act but rather amassed information in a thorough yet efficient manner before he made his plans and announced them. When General Crook gave his word he kept it, and everyone who was acquainted with him knew his word was good.

Crook had access to the complete record of physical evidence of the Wickenburg massacre, as well as Captain Meinhold's report. He had the support of the anti-Indian faction, which represented the majority of Arizona's settlers. He probably could have prosecuted the Indians right away and would have never heard more than a whimper of criticism, even from the easterners. Yet Crook chose to delay his premature conclusion and investigate the Wickenburg affair in his own meticulous manner.

Crook sent spies, white and Indian, into area towns and onto the reservations to gather intelligence about the identity of the per-petrators. While his spies worked, the general was approached by William Gilson,[26] who disclosed that he had strong reasons to believe the Date Creek Indians were responsible for the Wickenburg massacre. Gilson's ranch was located not only upon government property but within the Date Creek Reservation boundary. His ranch survived there because, as the *Miner* noted on September 14, 1872, "Mr. Gilson is a gentleman who has always responded to the wants of the aforesaid [Yavapai] savages." General Crook heard, in private, Gilson's testimony implicating the Indians, but there appears to be no written record of Gilson's reasons for placing the blame upon Date Creek's Yavapai Indians.

Capt. George Hall Burton[27] had been promoted only a few months prior to the attack, and, with his detachment, was assigned to the Colorado River Indian Reservation[28] to investigate reports of guilty Indians spending greenbacks there. The captain remained at the Colorado River Reservation from January 2 to May 31, 1872, gathering information. Captain Burton learned that the perpetrators, or at least a large number of them, had turned up on that reserva-tion shortly after the massacre, boasting of their deed, spending their greenbacks, and disposing of the few trinkets they had taken following the ambush.

There appears to be no written record of Captain Burton's find-ings, but the evidence available from the Colorado River Indian Reservation had been corroborated by Mohave Chief Irataba[29] and by Dr. John Alexis Tonner,[30] agent for that reservation. The evidence was reported to the Indian Bureau by Superintendent Herman Bendell[31] on December 23, 1871. Among the testimony was a description of the method of attack offered by the guilty Indians. The Apache-Mojave Indians bragged of fifteen Indians making the attack while fifteen more remained in hiding, but within hailing dis-tance ready to give aid.

On the day following the massacre, William Kruger reported to Captain Meinhold that he was "positive in his assertions that the attacking party were Indians." Then on December 9, 1871, in his letter to William Peckham he confirms the number of Indians involved when he wrote, "I counted and saw plainly fifteen Indians all dressed in blue soldiers' pants." Kruger's testimony corroborates the information later collected by Dr. Tonner, Chief Irataba, Captain Burton, and several Mohave Indians.

There was a report of two Indians dying on the reservation shortly after the attack, which coincided with Kruger's claim that he had "left his mark" on two Indians. That report was repeated in the Los Angeles *Daily News* on January 3, 1872: "Subsequent to the committal of the murder, two of the reservation Indians died of gunshot wounds, but whites were not permitted to see them."

The *Daily Alta California*, on November 25, 1871, reported, "These facts show conclusively that the Apache-Mohave, who have been fed, clothed and armed by the Government from the Camp Date Creek Reservation, are the guilty parties." But, the evidence had to be overwhelming before General Crook would move on the murderers and arrest them. He had civilians, Indians, government employees, and military staff involved in the investigation, which took many months. By the time the investigation was complete and to his satisfaction, he knew the guilty Indians by name and intended to turn the ringleaders over to civil authorities for trial. However, before he could execute his plan another peace commissioner—Gen. Oliver O. Howard[32]—arrived in Arizona and Gen. Crook was ordered to cease all actions against the hostile Indians.

After the massacre and throughout his investigation, General Crook had the support of the citizens in Arizona. Their confidence in him averted an incident which would have been as shocking and embarrassing as the Camp Grant Massacre, the April 1871 event when 150 men from Tucson attacked an Indian village and murdered

135 Indian women and children. The *San Bernardino Guardian* newspaper, always interested in Arizona's events, reprinted the following article on November 25, 1871:

A Movement Towards Vengeance

The Wickenburg Massacre nearly calls forth another horrible retribution on the heads of the murderers at the hands of our citizens. It is not surprising that the people of Arizona should have become well-nigh frenzied by the criminal courtesy shown the Assassins of the Indian Bureau; and the result of this frenzy would inevitably have been the *justifiable* murders of every Indian on the Date Creek Reservation, were it not for the complete confidence which the people have in Gen. Crook and which, at the eleventh hour, influenced them to let the matter rest in his hands feeling satisfied that he will do justice in the matter, so far as he has authority to act. No sooner had it been established beyond the possibility of mistake that the murder was perpetrated by Indians and that the Indians were in part, if not wholly, from the Date Creek Reservation, than a party of some sixty citizens was organized to take vengeance upon the murders, and soon declared itself in readiness to move.

About this time, a few members of the party—more thoughtful than their comrades—whose course we heartily commend, were instrumental in staying proceedings for the time, and timely in causing the abandonment of the project, through deference for the presence of Gen. Crook—knowing well that he would leave no means untried to have the matter properly attended to. And here let us add that this is not a case wherein justice can be done by simply killing the actual murderers, provided they should be discovered; there is not one Indian in the whole neighborhood, either on the reservation or elsewhere, who was not aware that the murder was to be perpetrated. These are all responsible—and the sacrifice of the worthless lives of the whole tribe would not compensate for the loss of the least one among the victims.

Support for General Crook continued in Arizona and California. In the January 27, 1872, edition of the *Arizona Citizen* (Tucson) the following was reported: "The Secretary of War fully approves of the administration of affairs in this Department by General Crook. So do all other sensible officers who have correct knowledge of his official conduct. General Crook always aims to do exactly right and rarely fails."

On March 23, 1872, California State Senator James McCoy of San Diego submitted a resolution to that state's Committee on Federal Relations including this excerpt:

Whereas we are fully aware that the following statements are true . . . that the feeling and belief is universal on the part of the Pacific slope that when General Crook was sent to Arizona he was the right man in the right place; that he is as humane as he is energetic, and that if allowed sufficient means and given the discretion to which his experience in the management of Indian affairs entitle him, and not inter-fered with in his operations, he will in a brief period arrest this reign of terror and blood and give security to the long-suffering people of the Territory.

By August 1872 General Crook's orders were changed again and he was free to pursue his plans. The orders issued on November 21, 1871, and published in the *Daily Alta California* on Christmas Eve were typical of the instructions under which Crook and other mili-tary leaders operated when dealing with their Indian charges:

HEADQUARTERS MILITARY DIVISION OF THE PACIFIC
San Francisco, Cal., November 21, 1871
General Order No. 10

In accordance with the authority and orders received from the War Department the following instructions are issued for the government of Indians, subject to Military control, in the Territory of Arizona:

All roving bands of Indians, for which reservations have been set apart by the Indian Commissioner under the authority of the President of the United States, will be required to go at once upon their reservations and not to leave them again upon any pretext whatever.

So long as they remain upon their reservations, in due subordination to the government, they will be fully protected and provided for. Otherwise, they will be regarded as hostile and punished accordingly.

The reservations heretofore set apart will be publicly declared in General Orders from Headquarters Department of Arizona, and an officer of the Army will be designated by the Department Commander to act as Indian Agent for each reservation. All male Indians (old enough to go upon the war-path) will be enrolled, and their names will be recorded in a book, kept for the purpose, with a full and accurate descriptive list of each person. Each Indian will be furnished with a copy of his descriptive list and will be required to carry it always with him.

The numbers of women and children belonging to each head of family will also be recorded opposite his name in the descriptive book.

The presence on the reservation of every male adult will be verified once a day, or oftener if found necessary, to prevent the possibility of any leaving the reservation and returning without the knowledge of the officer in charge. Care will be taken to inform the Indians that this precaution is intended to insure the protection of the innocent and punishment of the guilty, and that it is to their interest to assist in the detection of guilty individuals, so that the whole tribe may not suffer for the crimes of a few.

As far as possible the Indians will be held responsible only for their own individual acts. Punishment will not be inflicted upon a tribe, for the acts of individuals, unless they are guilty of complicity with the criminals by harboring them or otherwise. But when any enrolled Indian is found absent from his reservation, without permission, all his family will be arrested and held in close custody until he has been captured and punished according to his desserts.

Every Indian found off his reservation without permission, after a time to be fixed by the Department Commander, will be regarded and treated as hostile; and any Indian who shall so leave his reservation shall be presumed to have done so for hostile purposes, and upon his return to the reservation shall be arrested and punished accordingly. No Indian will be given permission to leave his reservation except upon such conditions as the Department Commander may prescribe.

No persons, excepting those in the United States service, will be allowed upon any Indian reservation without the permission of the officer in charge.

Citizens desiring to enter or cross a reservation for any legitimate purpose will, when it is deemed practicable and proper, be permitted to do so, but will always be escorted by sufficient detachment of troops to prevent any collision with the Indians.

The ration for issue to adult Indians will consist of one

pound of meat and one pound of breadstuff, two quarts of salt to each hundred rations, and four pounds of soap to a hundred rations once a week. Rations in half of the above proportions will be issued on the hoof. An officer will always be present to witness and direct the slaughtering of beef, and the distribution of food among the separate bands and families, and will certify to the Commanding Officer that it is fairly done.

The utmost care will be taken to see that rations are issued only for the number of Indians actually present, and that no opportunity is afforded for the barter of provisions for arms, ammunition, whiskey, or anything whatever.

Active operations will be kept up against the hostile Apaches of Arizona and pressed with all practicable vigor until they submit to the authority of the government, cease from hostilities and remain upon their reservations. After a reasonable time has been given for all the Apaches to avail themselves of the liberal terms offered by the government the Department Commander will, in his discretion, make use of the friendly Indians to hunt out and destroy those who remain obstinately hostile.

Full authority is conferred upon the Department Commander to adopt such measures as may be necessary to carry out these instructions, and to give full effect to the policy of the Government.

By Order of MAJOR-GENERAL SCHOFIELD:
J. C. Kelton, Assistant Adjutant General

Acting under General Order 10, General Crook arranged a council with the Indians upon the parade ground at Camp Date

Creek as a ploy to bring the massacre's ringleaders into his grasp. The General's report of the Date Creek Affair follows:

HEADQUARTERS DEPARTMENT OF ARIZONA
Prescott, September 18th, 1872
Assistant Adjutant General
Military Division of the Pacific
San Francisco, Cal.

Sir:

I have the honor to report that for some time I have been satisfied who the parties were who committed the massacre of the stage passengers near Wickenburg last November, in which Fred Loring and others lost their lives and have been keeping as quiet about it as possible while using every endeavor to get the individual Indians into position so as to capture them.

Having completed my arrangements, I left there on the 6th instant to meet Irataba, the Chief of the Mojaves, with an interpreter at Date Creek. The Chief was conversant of the massacre and the parties who committed it and was to identify such as were present at the council at Date Creek so that the arrest could be made.

On arriving at Date Creek I found that at least two thirds of the Indians belonging on the reservation were absent from it and that one band had left in a defiant manner stating that they were not coming back, while others had left with the permission of the agent to go to a certain place with the promise to come in whenever he sent for them, both of which promises they had failed to keep and in addition, several bands of which had stolen from parties on the road from Date Creek to Ehrenberg, the trails leading to the country over which these Indians were roaming.

The Indians who were at Date Creek seemed uneasy and suspicious and in very bad temper, appearing with their arms and warpaint. Some of the parties who had participated in the stage massacre were there, but very uneasy, and when the Indians were assembled I had some men detailed to make the arrests as soon as the Indians were identified. As they were designated, the soldiers stepped up to arrest them when one of the Indians' friends standing back of the soldiers stabbed one of them[33] in the back. A shot was fired, by whom I could hardly say, but I think it was the soldier stabbed, and in an instant firing commenced on both sides. The Indians making for the hills, I made every effort, as did all the officers present, to stop the firing but it was all over in an instant.

I returned to Prescott on the 9th and on the 10th inst. received a dispatch from the Commanding Officer of Date Creek stating that the Indians wanted to talk with me and I went down at once.

The Indians came in again and I promised them that I would grant amnesty to all the assassins except one of the ringleaders who was still at large as I had one in the guardhouse and two others were killed. Upon this nearly all the Indians I had met the first time came in again and said if I would allow them to remain they would be responsible for all the Indians who should come in. They did not deny their complicity with the stage massacre but said these men as good among bad Indians among them and that here of on they had been afraid to tell on each other when depredations were committed. They promised that hereafter they would not only tell me when any depredations were committed but they would go out with troops, if necessary, to punish the offenders.

As much as I regret that the arrest could not have been made without trouble I am well satisfied that, as it now happens, the affair will be productive of good as it is upon this basis and no other that you can rely upon Indians who come in upon our reservations.

The applications must come from them and not from us as they must sue to come in and not feel all this time that they confer a favor upon us by doing so.

Very respectfully,
Your Obedient Servant
George Crook
Lt. Col., 23rd Infantry
Brevet Maj. General
Commanding Department

It is telling to note that at no time throughout the period that General Crook pursued the perpetrators, did any Indian ever deny the involvement of Apache-Mojave Indians in the ambush.

A denial was eventually made, however. A claim for reparation was made by William Kruger in late 1874 against the San Carlos Indians. On January 3, 1875, U.S. Indian Agent John P. Clum,[34] who represented those Indians, reported that "the claim was submitted to the Indians, who denied the commission of the depredation." The Indians at San Carlos in late 1874 were justified in proclaiming their innocence. The tribe of guilty Indians—the Apache-Mojaves—did not begin their move to San Carlos until February 27, 1875.

Crook's spy network located the remainder of the guilty Indians, those not arrested or killed in the failed assassination of Gen. Crook, within a few weeks following the Date Creek Affair.

They had camped on Burro Creek in preparation for a raid on the Colorado River Indian Reservation to kill Chief Irataba. Within days after the guilty Indians were located, Capt. Julius Wilmot Mason[35] led Companies B, C, and K to the area of Muchos Cañons to attack the murderers in their four rancherias. Muchos Cañons was located at Burro Creek near the fork of the Big Sandy, the Santa Maria, and the Bill Williams Rivers, the latter formerly the Rio De San Andre River. Captain Mason filed the following report after the skirmish:

HEADQR'S DETACH'T FIFTH CAVALRY
September 24th, 1872
In the Field

> General George Crook,
> Commanding Dep't of Arizona, A.T.

> General: I have the honor to inform you that my command struck the Apache-Mohave Indians about daybreak this a.m. after a laborious march of eight (8) miles on foot over country literally cut up with deep cañons. Our surprise was a complete success, having attacked four (4) rancherias simultaneously, killing forty (40) Indians and wounding many more, also capturing eight (8) women and ten (10) children. The rancherias were on the brow of a deep cañon and to surround them was impossible, thus allowing some to escape who otherwise would have not.
> Officers and men behaved splendidly, and I cannot speak too highly of our Hualapai scouts. Their scouting was excellent, and when the fight came off they were not a bit behind the soldiers. I congratulate the commanding general

and the country in having secured so valuable an auxiliary. They are fully committed now. Guide Seaber [*sic*] did excellent service.

Please inform me, as soon as possible, what disposition shall be made of the captured women and children. Four (4) ponies were captured and turned over to the Indians.

I return to Hualapai by easy marches tomorrow. The fearful foot marching has made us all foot-sore. The Indians were found at the place designated in the accompanying letter, handed me by you while at Hualapai.

> Very respectfully, your ob't serv't,
> J. W. Mason
> Capt. 5th Cav. Com'g Detachment

General Crook continued to receive support. An article from the *San Francisco Chronicle*, republished in the *Miner* on March 22, 1873, summarized feelings about the General:

General Crook, commanding the Territory of Arizona, is an officer of experience and discretion. He has the military capacity to conquer these Indians and he has the judgment, while he punishes the guilty, to spare the innocent. Our advice to the Government is to allow General Crook to make war upon these hostile Indians and not to interfere with him or send preachers to him, nor hamper him with restrictions. Let him punish these red devils till they recognize the power of our Government, and till they forbear in the course of plunder and murder in which for many years they have been engaged. Arizona is a rich and productive region; it is kept desolate and depopulated because there is no security for life. Tenderness and mercy to the Indian is death to the white people, and the sooner a thousand Apache warriors are killed the better it will be for society and civilization.

Capt. John G. Bourke published *On the Border with Crook* in 1891 and provided the best summary of the feelings that persisted about the General. He wrote:

There never was an officer in our military service so completely in accord with all the ideas, views, and opinions of the savages whom he had to fight or control as was General Crook. In time of campaign this knowledge placed him, as it were, in the secret councils of the enemy; in time of peace it enabled him all the more completely to appreciate the doubts and misgivings of the Indians at the outset of a new life, and to devise plans by which they could all the more readily be brought to see that civilization was something which all could embrace without danger of extinction. But while General Crook was admitted, even by the Indians, to be more of an Indian than the Indian himself, it must in no wise be understood that he ever occupied any other relation than that of the older more experienced brother who was always ready to hold out a helping hand to the younger just learning to walk and climb. Crook never ceased to be a gentleman. . . . His voice was always low, his conversation easy, and his general bearing one of quiet dignity.

Post returns for Camp Whipple[36] and Camp Date Creek from September 26, 1871, through October 24, 1872, shed some light on the happenings at these two military posts during the time after the massacre:

Camp Whipple (HQ) Returns

Sept. 26, 1871. George H. Burton promoted to Captain.

December, 1871. George H. Burton "on detached service at Regimental HQ"; Order #90, Captain Burton ordered to join his Company.

January 2, 1872. instruction to Captain G. H. Burton, 21st Infantry relative to detachment under his command inst. to Captain G. H. Burton directing him to proceed to Colorado River Reservation. [where he investigated the claim that the guilty Indians had been there bragging of their attack on the stagecoach and selling their meager plunder]

June 24, 1872. Captain George H. Burton returned to duty on orders dated May 31, 1872, per HQ.

July 23, 1872. Captain George H. Burton transferred to San Francisco, CA; left post August 2, 1872. [having completed his investigative duties]

October, 1872. General Order #32 announces the success of a scout against hostile Indians commanded by Captain J. W. Mason, 5th Cavalry.

Date Creek Camp Returns

November 12, 1871. letter "relative to the late attack upon the stage near Wickenburg, Ariz."

September, 1872: Sept. 2. Apache-Mojave Indian *Ocho-Cama* and *Hock-A-Che-Waka* left the reservation on pass.

Department Commander informed of this fact. *Sept. 6*, Capt. Byrne, 13th Infantry arrived from Camp Beale Springs, A.T. *Irataba* and other Mojave and Hualpai Indians. *Sept 7.* Dispatch received *3 O'cl. a.m.* announcing the stealing of stock from *Cullings Station*. Sent scouting party in pursuit. Received news of the defection of the bands of *Ocho-Cama* and *Hock-A-Che-Waka*, arrested and confined *Tee-Yee-Made-Yee* (brother of *Ocho-Cama*) and *"Indian Jim"* as hostages to secure the return of their bands. Department Commander arrived a.m. *Sept. 8* Grand Conference of the Department Commander and Superintendent of Indian Affairs in Arizona with the Chiefs of the *Apache-Yumas* and *Apache-Mojaves*. Arrest of Indian criminals *Ocho-Cama*, *What-E-Ora-Ma*, *Chimhueva Sal*, and *Ah-Pook-Ya* by orders of the Department Commander after the conference. Resistance by the criminals and attack of the Indians upon the guards, in which one of the latter was severely—if not fatally—stabbed by an Indian. Escape of *Chimhueva Sal* from the guard and killing of *What-E-Ora-Ma* whilst escaping. Attempted escape from the guardhouse at the same time by the Indian prisoners confined on the 7th inst.—Department Commander, Capt. Byrne and the Indians brought by the latter departed 8 p.m.—all the Indians left the reservation. *Sept. 9, 4 O'Clock a.m.* Desperate and successful attempt at escape by *Ocho-Cama* and *Indian Jim* though both seriously—if not mortally—wounded by the guards. Killing of *Tee-Yee-Made-Yee* whilst attempting to escape at the same time. Burial of killed and bringing in of wounded Indians found in the vicinity of the post (Department Comd. informed unofficially). *Sept. 11, Chimhueva Jim* captured near post and restored— unharmed—to his tribe with messages to *Jem-As-Pie*, Chief of the *Apache-Yumas*. Courier sent with dispatches to

Department Commander. *Sept. 12, Jem-As-Pie* with a portion of his tribe came into post. Rations issued them. Department Commander informed. *Sept. 13, Capt. Hinton* and officers and 23rd Infantry arrived a.m. *Department Commander* arrived p.m. *Sept. 14, Column of 23rd Infantry* arrived. Conference of Department Commander with Indians a.m. *Sept. 15,* Command of Post assumed by *Captain James Hinton,* 23rd infantry. *Sept. 16,* "A," "G" and "K" companies of *23rd Infantry* left for their resp. stations. Interview between the Department Commander and *Jem-As-Pie* Indians. *Jem-As-Pie* promises to come into the reservation next day. Department Commander left for Prescott in the afternoon. *Sept. 17, Jem-As-Pie* failed to come upon the reservation with his Indians according to promise. The fact reported to Dept. Commander and instructions asked.

General Crook was a man of impeccable honesty and integrity, but more importantly a man who respected and protected the "good" Indians under his care. He was also a man who insisted on being thorough to a certainty before he would pursue a punitive action. He refused to accept the proposition that "one Indian is as good as another," and insisted that the ringleaders be identified. He intended to punish only the guilty, and after months of tedious investigation he moved to capture rather than kill them.

Chapter 6
Who Didn't?

MEXICANS

"The Wickenburg Horror; Murder and Robbery on the Highway; Were They Indians or Mexicans?" was the headline in the *Miner* on September 11, 1871. There had not been sufficient time to imagine the twists and turns that would later convolute the correct placement of blame. But, there was time to capitalize upon a warning issued months earlier in Wickenburg.

In early September 1871 a Mexican woman said she was passing near the exterior wall of a brush shack and overheard two Mexican ruffians, one a relative, discussing plans to rob a stagecoach. This prompted her to warn George "Crete" Bryan, who regularly took his meals at her place, to avoid taking the stagecoach west from Wickenburg. She warned no others of the impending robbery, and that would have been the end of this tale if a stagecoach had not been attacked and robbed two months later.

George Bryan was a member of the pursuit posse which went in search of the murderers. He affixed his name to the "Corrected Account of the Massacre" that appeared in the *Miner*. In that statement he unequivocally laid blame upon the Apache-Mojave Indians of Date Creek. However, Charles B. Genung later reported that Bryan confided in him that he (Bryan) doubted it was the Indians. Genung reported that Bryan believed it could have been Mexicans that attacked the stagecoach.

Mexican bandits had been active north of the border for years, and there were those who would profit if the Indians were exonerated and the Mexicans were blamed. The first effort in that direction was to implicate the Mexican ranchers and wood choppers from the Hassayampa Cañon. Quickly, however, attention was shifted to the numerous bandits and rowdies known to be in the area. There was always a sufficient number of vagrant Mexicans hanging around every southwestern settlement to absorb the blame for sordid deeds.

It was Charles B. Genung who was at the hub of this controversy. Genung had always been a friend and protector of the Indians, whom he exploited to build his roads. Each day he would work his Indians from daylight to dark and pay them fifty cents for their efforts. If not for the opportunity to exploit the Indians in that manner, Genung's roads would have cost him at least three times as much to build. He had much to gain by shifting the blame from the Yavapai Indians to the Mexicans.

In his memoirs Genung reported the tale of Donya Tomase bringing a relative, named Parenta, into her home and plying him with wine until he told her the names of the perpetrators and the circumstances of the stagecoach ambush and murders. Conveniently, Parenta had been sick on the day the massacre occurred and thus had not participated. Though one of the planners, he was not targeted by Genung for punishment.

Through Tomase's tale, Genung claimed that he knew the names of some of the perpetrators. He proceeded to whisper them to a circle of trusted friends, never publishing them outright, allegedly to protect Donya Tomase. The people who were privy to the names, according to Genung, were John Burger, George Bryan, James Grant, Phoenix Deputies Joe Phy (sometimes misspelled Tye or Fye) and Milt Ward, and Phoenix citizens George Updyke and "Doc" Park.

John Burger, armed with the names of the supposed attackers, shot and killed a Mexican in a corral at Agua Fria. According to

Genung, Burger accused the Mexican of being an assassin. The Mexican drew his knife and attacked Burger, even though Burger was armed with a pistol.

Deputies Joe Phy and Milt Ward went to Agua Fria and arrested a wounded Mexican on an unrelated charge. When the man was knifed to death in his Phoenix jail cell by a fellow inmate, Genung's inner circle put their fingers to their lips, as they were inclined to do occasionally, and then expressed pleasure that another assassin got what he deserved. But the Phoenix deputies were not through yet. They escorted Joaquin Barbe and a companion outside the town's limits where the two Mexicans were killed during an argument. Once again two names were added to Genung's list, posthumously.

Another name posthumously added to the list was Ramon Cordova—the Mexican who reportedly gave a watch fob to a "soiled dove" in Wickenburg. He was arrested on June 1, 1872, and the *Miner* reported: "A few days ago Sheriff T. C. Warden, assisted by Joseph Fye [*sic*] at the house of King S. Woolsey, Agua Caliente, succeeded in capturing Ramon Cordovo [*sic*], one of the Mexicans implicated in the Wickenburg stage massacre. Of this fact the Sheriff has undoubted proof. He was safely lodged in jail on Monday afternoon. On Wednesday evening some person or persons, unknown, broke into the jail, cut the shackles which fastened said Corvodo [*sic*] to his cell, and hanged him in the jail."

Deputy Phy, of Genung's inner circle of confidants, was involved in the arrest and possibly responsible for implicating Cordova in the Wickenburg massacre. He may have even been involved in the lynching. The "undoubted proof" implicating Cordova in the massacre was not shared in the article, but the *Miner* continued: "Yesterday morning a coroner's jury found a verdict in accordance with the above facts." However, the proof implicating Cordova in the massacre was never revealed.

After Cordova was dead Juan Reval was arrested. He had been

convicted of murder in Phoenix and faced a life sentence in the territorial prison in Yuma. Genung visited Reval in his jail cell and bribed him with whiskey that he had smuggled into the jail. Genung later reported that Reval had revealed the complicity of a number of individuals. There was no written record of the confession or other witnesses to substantiate Juan Reval's statements.

Eventually there was a lull in the deaths of Mexican rowdies, and Genung announced that one of the perpetrators had fled to Mexico while, conveniently, the others had gone underground. They were never named or sought out for punishment. Genung, it seems, simply lost interest in seeking revenge on local Mexicans.

The total number of Mexicans on Genung's list of perpetrators grew from two men planning a stagecoach robbery behind the walls of a brush shack in early September to ten men on November 5, 1871. If Genung's numbers were correct, it must be presumed that at least three of the Mexicans were able to aim two heavy, single-shot rifles with deadly accuracy and then reload both in the time it takes the average man to load one, since by the most conservative estimates there were twenty-six bullets discharged in two volleys requiring thirteen long arms.

Furthermore, ammunition was readily available to Mexicans in any quantities, so it seems highly unlikely that Mexican ambushers would have taken only two rounds apiece to the scene of the crime. In addition, the alleged Mexican perpetrators would have had to spend time and effort collecting a variety of objects to plant along the trail, including some not easily obtainable, and then dress in blue cavalry pants even though they expected there would be no witnesses to testify to the clothing they wore. Finally, the Wells Fargo box was left untouched and most of the mail unopened. Captain Meinhold reported: "I ascertained that no horses were stolen, nor any baggage. That even persons of the passengers were not searched and robbed except Mr. Adams whose pockets were found to be turned inside out."

Charles Genung refused to accept the findings of General Crook, but the evidence and related scenarios do not support his claim that the Mexicans were responsible. Too many of the discrepancies cannot be resolved to implicate the Mexicans.

WHITES

The original statement that whites may have been involved came from Ms. Mollie Sheppard. Her reasoning was that she had heard, secondhand, that men in Prescott had asked about the time of her departure and how much money she might have had with her.

Ms. Sheppard had just spent several years battling the Yavapai County Board of Supervisors over taxation on her house and they had finally succeeded in driving her from Prescott. It is not unreasonable that she might be suspicious of the men of Prescott. However, the questions asked about her, if they were asked, were as likely to have come from regular clients concerned about her welfare as from those she had helped over the years. Though Mollie Sheppard was only twenty-four years old, she had spent a great deal of time and her own money caring for the sick and the poor of Prescott.

SURVIVORS

There has been conjecture that the survivors—Sheppard and Kruger—were behind the robbery. This scenario would have William Kruger drawing a rifle within the cramped quarters of the coach, killing several passengers inside while leaving one unharmed and another wounded. Then Kruger would have had to alight from the coach and kill two armed and alerted men on top of the coach. This is hardly plausible.

Loring, the third man riding atop, was unarmed though he had been offered a gun by Kruger at the outset of the journey. This scenario would have required Kruger and Ms. Sheppard to run about the coach shooting it full of holes from all angles with long arms and ammunition that they did not possess. Kruger and Ms. Sheppard would have then had to bury the loot in the desert and then wound each other several times to give their story credibility.

The story of Kruger and Sheppard as the robbers is entirely contradictory of the physical evidence, but began because of rumors that Kruger had been stealing from the army. It was alleged that he carried thousands of dollars in stolen money, and that the robbery was intended to cover up the loss. If he had been stealing and had the money with him, it is difficult to imagine how having it stolen a second time, by Indians, would actually cover up the first theft.

Another report suggests that Kruger was carrying a large payroll, perhaps as much as one hundred thousand dollars. However, whenever the army moved large amounts of money, it sent an escort of at least four men. There was no escort with the stagecoach that day.

Yet another report indicated that a "short, stocky man dressed like a prospector" was killed by a stray bullet during a saloon brawl in Phoenix, Arizona, in December 1872. The man had registered in a nearby hotel as William Kruger, and it was inferred that this man was the survivor of the massacre who had returned to dig up the stolen money. However, after the date of this reported death, Kruger filed an affidavit in Ohio for his depredation claim to recover the money stolen from him. William Kruger's signature appears on claim documents as late as December 4, 1875. The prospector killed in a Phoenix saloon could not have been the same William Kruger.

Captain O'Beirne, commanding Camp Date Creek, wrote in a letter to the *Army and Navy Journal* published on March 2, 1872, that William Kruger was discharged from his army duties by Col. Charles Warren Foster. He also wrote that during Kruger's stay in Ehrenberg, his brother Frederick would not speak with him if they passed on the street. O'Beirne was incorrect and, in fact, Frederick

Kruger sent his brother a letter which arrived in San Francisco before William Kruger's arrival on January 11, 1872. As well, Frederick sought out his brother in person in February 1872 to offer him extended employment in Colonel Foster's command. William Kruger continued his employment in Ehrenberg until November 1872. So much effort was expended to re-employ William Kruger that one would hardly suspect there was even the faintest hint of impropriety on his part.

Charles Genung, who reportedly held an intense dislike for all Mexicans, did everything he could to shift the blame from the Indians he exploited to build roads. All the evidence, however, when carefully analyzed, excludes Mexicans as the perpetrators of the massacre. Nor could the blame be placed upon the Whites— Sheppard's paranoia is not enough evidence. The suggestion that the survivors were responsible is worse than implausible; the idea is almost laughable. By the simple process of elimination we come full circle, albeit by a circuitous route, to the conclusion that the Date Creek Reservation Indians were responsible for the Wickenburg massacre.

The Arizona census of 1870 reports Mollie Sheppard's birthplace as Ireland and her age as twenty-three years old. This would place her birth year as 1847, during the Irish potato famine. The Sheppard clan is primarily from the town of Clifton in County Tipperary, though a few Sheppards were reported to reside in Wexford during that period.

The only record of a Ms. Sheppard arriving in San Francisco is aboard the *Lyme Regis*, a three-masted barque. According to this record, Ms. Sheppard left London on June 18, 1852, and was at sea one hundred thirty-nine days. The *Lyme Regis* sailed around the Cape of Good Hope and across the north coast of Australia. Twenty miles north of Flattery Point, off the eastern shore of the continent, Captain W. Scott located Cook's Passage through the Great Barrier Reef and piloted his vessel into a sheltered cove at Lizard Island. The *Lyme Regis* continued its voyage east and docked off North Beach outside San Francisco, California, on November 16, 1852. Mollie would have been just five years old when she was sent, unescorted by family, to America.

The passenger list for the *Lyme Regis* is consistent with a passage by sea of a small girl traveling alone. The list consisted of three young "Misses"—Ms. Hatch, Ms. Reynolds, and Ms. Sheppard. The captain's wife "with child" and a "Mrs. Schonidt with son" were the only other passengers listed on the register. The captain, apparently, took his pregnant wife along to supervise and care for the three young girls. Mrs. Schonidt may also have been along to care for the girls and perhaps to care for Mrs. Scott as well. Or she may have simply been an additional, compatible passenger.

Coincidentally George Crook, a recent graduate from the military academy, passed through San Francisco two weeks after Ms. Sheppard arrived. He was en route to his first assignment.

The next mention of Mollie Sheppard is in the 1870 census. Reports indicate that by 1871 she had been embroiled in a battle for nearly three years with the Yavapai County Board of Supervisors over a tax issue. Thus, Mollie can be verified as a resident of Prescott, Arizona Territory, since 1868. By then she was established as a successful prostitute. Whether the Yavapai County Board drove her out or she elected to leave Prescott, Mollie sold her business and home and left Prescott on Saturday morning, November 4, 1871. Her immediate destination was San Francisco.

During the Sunday morning attack upon the Wickenburg-Ehrenberg stagecoach Mollie Sheppard received three wounds. She had two slight wounds to her back and one serious wound to her right arm. It was the wound to her right arm that required her to stay at the laundress's quarters at Camp Date Creek for a short time. While there, Mrs. Ebstein,[37] the only officer's wife at the post, offered her clothing and any other assistance she might need, a compassionate gesture considering Ms. Sheppard's social status. Later, Ms. Sheppard was moved to Gilson's ranch[38] where, for at least several weeks, she recuperated until she could resume her travels.

Dr. David Jones Evans,[39] in his letter to the *Army and Navy Journal* published on March 2, 1872, described her condition:

On my arrival at Wickenburg I found the only survivors, Mr. Kruger and Ms. Sheppard, wounded; Kruger slightly, and the woman badly in the upper third right arm.

Having been informed that no proper medical aid could be procured at the latter place, and in consultation with Captain Meinhold in regard to the matter, we came to the conclusion to remove them to a point near Camp Date Creek where they would receive proper care and attention. On our arrival at the post, it being near dark the woman was placed in the quarters occupied by the hospital matron, until such time as arrangements could be made for her removal to Mr. Gilson's, on the reservation, (2½) miles from camp.

On visiting her the morning after her arrival, I found her arm much swollen and inflamed, and so reported to you, when I was ordered to keep her there until such time as she could be removed without harm to herself to more comfortable quarters.

Also, that I should admit William Kruger to hospital for treatment, etc., he refusing to go into hospital and preferring to remain at the matron's with the wounded woman until such time as she had recovered sufficiently to be removed to Mr. Gilson's where he accompanied her and where they remained until entirely recovered.

Splinters from the stagecoach body were embedded in Mollie's right arm, which wasn't healing properly. The body of a Concord stagecoach is made of wood. The wood is painted and rubbed out with pumice before two layers of spar varnish are applied. This combination of materials and residue, aggravated by the constant reopening of the wound, could have led to blood poisoning.

The Los Angeles *Daily News*, on January 3, 1872, reported: "The unfortunate woman's arm is still unhealed, the foreign matter not having been extracted. A piece of painted wood, being a portion of the stagecoach, worked its way out of the wound a few days ago." That reopening of the wound occurred just before Ms.

Sheppard's arrival in San Bernardino on December 30, 1871.

The *San Bernardino Guardian* reported: "The La Paz stage arrived Thursday evening, bringing among the passengers from Arizona the only two survivors of the Wickenburg Stage Massacre, Mr. W. Kruger and Ms. Sheppard. The former has recovered from his wounds, the latter is not so fortunate, as her wounds have not yet healed."

On May 23, 1874, the *Arizona Citizen* (Tucson) posted the following notice, which must have been sent to their attention by telegraph:[40] "Prescott, May 21—Wm. Kruger is now the sole survivor of the Wickenburg stage massacre. Ms. Sheppard having died soon after the attack of her wounds, at least so Mr. Kruger recently informed the editor of Crofutt's *Western World*, which paper is wrong in stating that Kruger is of the army."

The Crofutt's article referred to was published in the May 1874 edition and titled, "Chat with Correspondents." The editor described the column as one "in which department questions of all sorts will receive attention, and for which facts of interest are solicited." An eastern correspondent had requested the date of the murder of Fred W. Loring, and the editor of the *Miner* responded to Croffut's editor with the date, who then wrote: "As we write this, Captain Kruger, who is sitting in the World office, substantiates the above [referring to the *Miner* response]. He was really the only survivor, Miss Sheppard having died of her wounds soon after the massacre. Should our questioner desire an interview with Captain Kruger in regard to the matter he can do so by calling at the Park Hotel. . . . He [Kruger] is now in the East on leave of absence until July next, prosecuting his claim for loss against the government, and, we are happy to learn, with every prospect of success."

Kruger had, previous to the *Croffut* and *Citizen* articles, filed an affidavit to recover his losses. In it he mentions Mollie Sheppard, but does not mention her death. Kruger swore and subscribed before

Notary Public A. B. Heychum on March 11, 1873, that "himself and another passenger, Ms. Mollie Shep[p]ard only escap[ed] with their lives." This first effort at recovery failed.

Mr. Kruger continued in his efforts to recover the money supposedly stolen from him and filed another affidavit on October 25, 1874, before Notary Public Louis Ritter in Cleveland, Ohio. This time he swore and subscribed "and that he and Ms. Shephard [sic] were the only survivors, both severely wounded, that Ms. Shephard [sic] died soon after in consequence of her wounds, and that he is now the only survivor of the so-called 'Loring' or Wickenburg Massacre."

The first mention of Ms. Sheppard's death in the affidavits came nearly twenty-nine months after she was alleged to have succumbed to her wounds. The second report came five months later. Is it any wonder that the editor of the *Citizen* registered disbelief?

After the events of the massacre, Mollie Sheppard began her first trip west on November 4, 1871. William Kruger was in her company, but his destination was Ehrenberg, where he had employment through the end of that year. Mollie was planning to continue on. Had her plans included setting up a household in Ehrenberg, or elsewhere on the West Coast, she would have retained her household goods and taken them with her. But, in the October 21, 1871, edition of the *Miner* the following notice appeared:

AUCTION SALE
Friday, October 27, 1871
At 11 O'Clock a.m.

All the FURNITURE, BEDDING, COOKING UTEN-SILS, CROCKERY, GLASSWARE, &c., belonging to the undersigned, will be sold to the highest bidders, for cash, at her residence, Montezuma Street, Prescott. Also, one good saddle horse.

MOLLIE SHEPARD [sic]

Mollie's itinerary had her leaving Wickenburg on November fifth and arriving in Ehrenberg on the sixth, arriving in San Bernardino by the evening of the seventh, and then arriving in Los Angeles on the evening of the eighth. Her ship, the *Orizaba*, was scheduled to leave Los Angeles on the twelfth and was scheduled to arrive in San Francisco on November fourteenth. Her arrival was just three days before the regularly scheduled Pacific Mail Steamship Company's steamship departed for Panama City. While in Los Angeles in January of 1872, Ms. Sheppard and William Kruger were interviewed and stated that their destination was Washington, D. C. The full text of that interview follows.

LOS ANGELES DAILY NEWS—
January 3, 1872
The Wickenburg Massacre
The Survivors Interviewed
Their Thrilling Narrative of the Affair

The fiendish massacre of the stage passengers near Wickenburg by the bloodthirsty Apaches on the 4th of last November, is still fresh in the memory of all. The only survivors—Ms. Mollie Sheppard and Mr. W. Kruger—are now sojourning in this city, awaiting the sailing of the next steamer to convey them to San Francisco, *en route* to Washington, their destination. Yesterday, a reporter of the News called upon them, and received a thrilling account of their hairbreadth escape from their own lips. Mr. Kruger is a bright intelligent young man of German extraction, very light in complexion, and rather below the medium height in stature, but of very strong frame. Ms. Sheppard is a tall lady, of prepossessing manner and appearance. The wounds she then received have not yet fully healed, as she still carries her right arm in a sling.

MASSACRE at Wickenburg

THE ATTACK

The party occupying the stage at the time of its leaving Wickenburg were in high spirits and anticipated no danger of an attack. Their arms had been stored beneath the cushions of the seats for convenience and safety; and wit, wine, and humor flowed freely; everything went on as "merry as a marriage bell" until the moment of attack. Ms. Sheppard and Mr. Kruger, with some of the others, sat on the inside. Young Loring rode on the outside, in the company of the driver. The first notification the inside passengers had of the presence of danger, was at a point about nine miles from Wickenburg, when they were startled by the voice of the driver calling out "Apaches! Apaches! Apaches!" Scarcely was the alarm thus given than a volley was discharged from the rifles of the savages into the stage coach, succeeded almost instantly by a second one. The driver, Loring, Shoholm, and Hamel were killed instantly, Loring groaning slightly for a few moments, Hamel and Shoholm remaining upright in their seats. Mr. Salmon received a shot in the abdomen, and, seemingly in his agony, sprang out of the stage. Mr. Kruger received a ball in his right shoulder, and two shots in the back. Upon the firing of the first volley he grasped Ms. Sheppard and forced her under the seat, lying down on the floor of the coach himself, having previously discharged the contents of his pistol into their [the Indians'] midst. Ms. Sheppard had been wounded in the right arm above the elbow, and two shots had ploughed through the flesh of her shoulder. After the discharge of the second volley, everything remained quiet for a few moments, so still that the dropping of a pin might have been distinctly heard. There being no signs of life in the coach, the savages presumed that they had succeeded in killing all, and with one accord sprang cat-like from their ambush upon the coach.

When within almost arm's length of it, Mr. Kruger and Ms. Sheppard sprang to their feet and yelled with all their might, the former holding his revolver in their faces. This was too much for the cowardly redskins, and they at once retreated pell-mell to cover. The two then sprang from the stage and called out for all of those still alive to follow them. The only response was from Mr. Adams who was lying on the bottom of the coach. Adams seemed to have been paralyzed by the shot he had received, being unable to move anything except his head, which he raised saying, "O God, can't you save me!" When asked if he could move, he answered in the negative, and Kruger then told him that they would be compelled to leave him to his fate. He was then lying face downwards. When subsequently found, he had been turned over, and shot through the head.

THEIR FLIGHT

The two then left the stage and struck through the brush, closely followed by the Indians. The Apaches had apparently expended their rifle ammunition at the first attack, as they had pistols only when following the fugitive. These they discharged at them frequently, keeping, however, at a respectable distance, dreading the revolver in the hand of Kruger, which was leveled at them whenever they attempted to close upon them. Ms. Sheppard had also armed herself with an empty whiskey bottle furnished to her by Kruger, which also had considerable effect in intimidating them when they approached, mistaking it for a weapon. Shortly afterward, they regained the road, and plodded along in the direction of Ehrenberg, dogged by four Apaches on the right and five on the left. Kruger all the while supporting his companion with one hand, and intimidating their pursuers with the revolver in the other. Their wounds were bleeding freely during the whole time and, when completely exhausted, having traveled through loose sand for a distance of at least five miles, they were greeted by the welcome sight of a cloud of dust arising from the buckboard conveying mails to Wickenburg. The Apaches were not any slower than themselves in discovering it, and almost immediately vanished. The driver of the buckboard was so frightened, when he saw the fugitives, that it was with some difficulty that he was induced to take them on board, and even then, not until Kruger threatened to shoot him. They were then conveyed a few miles in the direction of Ehrenberg, to the confines of a barren desert, some thirty or forty miles broad, on the other side of which that city lay. Here the driver concluded to leave them, while he rode across the country for assistance, leaving them a keg, which he professed to be half full of water, and promising to return by seven o'clock in the evening. An improvised barricade was formed of the mail bags and a trunk, behind which they remained, fearing momentarily another attack from the Apaches. It was not until past midnight that relief came. In the interim, they had suffered fearfully from thirst and cold, having discovered that the keg was completely dry, and fearing to kindle a fire lest it might attract the Indians. At eleven o'clock they saw, in the form of fires, signs on the hills which satisfied them that there was succor coming. A body of about twenty armed men, with an ambulance to convey the dead, had been brought from Wickenburg, and they, with five of the six that had been murdered, were at once taken back to that place. The sixth body—that of Mr. Salmon—was not found until the following morning as he had crawled some distance away from the stage, where he had fallen into the hands of the savages and been scalped, the skin being torn off from the chin to the back of the head.

WHERE THE DEAD WERE BURIED

Loring, Shoholm, Hamel, and Adams were all decently buried at Wickenburg, but Salmon was interred in the middle of the road near where the attack had been made. And so little pains were taken to bury him that portions of his remains were still exposed above the surface. What portion of his body the coyotes could get at they stripped the bones clear of the flesh. When the survivors passed the scene on their way here, the bare bones projected above ground. The scoundrels who undertook to do this last act of charity to the dead had the audacity to charge the estate $95 for the job, that being the amount of cash found on the dead man's person.

MONEY AND VALUABLES LOST

The Indians had rifled all the baggage within the stage, taking therefrom all the valuables they contained in the way of money and jewelry. Kruger's loss is within a trifle of $8,000 and Ms. Sheppard's a similar amount. The other passengers also had large sums of money, all of which the miscreants had carried away.

WHY THE MAILS WERE NOT RANSACKED

The mailbags were packed in the boot of the stage. A demijohn containing about a gallon of whiskey, six bottles of Jamaica Rum, and several bottles of porter, were stowed there also. After ransacking one or two of the bags, it is presumed that the Apaches discovered the liquor, and abandoned everything for it, leaving the balance of the mail untouched in the forgetfulness of intoxication.

WHO THE MURDERERS WERE

The survivors are confident that the murderers were Apache-Mojaves from the Camp Date Creek Reservation. They had on the blue pants worn by the reservation Indians, and had the gait, appearance and bearing of the Apaches during the whole time they were under their observation, which it would have been impossible for any Whites or Mexicans to have assumed and maintained. In addition to this, Captain Winhold of the 3rd Cavalry, who had been detailed to find out, if possible, who they were, followed the tracks in the direction of Camp Date Creek. The footprints were round-toed after the manner of the Apaches. On the trail a reservation hunting bag was picked up, and a pack of cards, with corners cut off, such as are used by the Apache-Mojaves. He declared, in his report to his superior, that it was his firm conviction that the murderers were Camp Date Creek Apaches. Furthermore, subsequent to the committal of the murder, two of the reservation Indians died of gunshot wounds; but Whites were not permitted to see them. The Reservation Indians have also purchased ammunition from the soldiery, giving greenbacks in denominational value of $10 and $20 in payment therefore. While Kruger was at Ehrenberg, he received information that Apaches were offering $20 and $50 greenbacks at La Paz, five miles distant, for $2.00 coin. He repaired thither, and while there was seen by an Apache, who seemed to recognize him instantly and with a yell disappeared. All the Apaches in that neighborhood left immediately afterwards. The survivors are confident that had Colonel O'Byrne [sic], the Commandant of the Reservation, caused the Indians there to undergo a strict search immediately after obtaining information of the massacre, that the property would have been discovered in their possession.

HOW THE SURVIVORS WERE TREATED

The wounded man and woman were taken to Camp Date Creek to receive medical treatment, Dr. Evans being the only physician nearer than Ehrenberg. Colonel O'Byrne [sic], the inhuman Commandant of the Camp, ordered Ms. Sheppard, however, to leave on account of her being an unfortunate. Kruger had claims upon the hospitalities of the Camp other than that naturally due to one in distress, as he was in Government employ, being Chief Clerk and Cashier of Colonel Foster, Quartermaster, stationed at Prescott. He removed Ms. Sheppard to Gilson's ranch, about two miles from the post, and there put up his own quarters, the doctor paying them daily visits. His bill for attendance upon Ms. Sheppard, during the fifteen days she remained there, amounted to $570, which he subsequently reduced to $300 in gold coin. The unfortunate woman's arm is still unhealed, the foreign matter not having been extracted. A piece of painted wood, being a portion of the stagecoach, worked its way out of the wound a few days ago.

RELICS

The lady carries with her relics of the tragedy in the form of a fur cape, which contains as many as nine bullet holes. The old hat worn by Loring at the time of his untimely death has been forwarded to his father, that being all that was left of his effects unrobbed or unburied. The two survivors are now on their way to Washington, where Mr. Kruger is in hopes that he will recover, at least, his property, as he was traveling at the time on Government duty.

The *Orizaba* left Los Angeles a day late on January 8, but due to a violent Pacific storm bypassed the wayport of Santa Barbara and arrived in San Francisco an additional day late on January 11, 1872. Mollie Sheppard and William Kruger checked into the American Exchange Hotel on January 11, and that was the last word of Sheppard's whereabouts. It appears they separated company at about that time, which would be consistent with her departing for Panama City, Panama.

William Kruger learned that a letter was waiting for him when he arrived in San Francisco. He remained in San Francisco until his brother joined him in February. Kruger then reestablished his army employment in March, which continued through November 1872.

Conjecture suggests that the American Exchange Hotel was selected by Kruger because of its proximity to the German section of San Francisco, since he was German. Other evidence suggests that it may have been chosen by Ms. Sheppard because of its proximity to the red-light district, where Sheppard might have had business contacts, or Chinatown where she might have purchased herbs and potions for her wound. Proximity to the German section does not seem a priority, however, since Kruger's brother, Frederick,[41] chose the Cosmopolitan Hotel for his accommodations in February. It was not necessary to be near any particular part of San Francisco in 1872 since transportation was readily available throughout that metropolis.

The American Exchange Hotel, located at 319 to 325 Sansome Street, has one important distinction. It was within one mile of the wharf office of the Pacific Mail Steamship Company at First and Brannan Streets, from which steamships for Panama City were scheduled on the third and seventeenth of each month.

It was clear from the January 2 interview that Ms. Sheppard initially intended on taking the normal route to the East Coast, ultimately ending the first leg of her trip in Washington, D. C. Mollie's rush to San Francisco, even though she was not fully healed and in pain, may be explained by her need to connect with the steamship *Alaska*.

In 1855 the forty-eight-mile-long trans-isthmus railway was completed between Panama City on the west coast and Aspinwall on the east coast of Panama along the same approximate route that the Panama Canal would be built decades later. From that time it was not necessary to sail around Cape Horn, or to trek across Nicaragua or Panama by horse or mule to reach the opposite coast of the United States. Either route was treacherous.

After 1855 eastbound travelers sailed to Panama City, boarded the train for the east coast of Panama, and then boarded another steamer at Aspinwall to sail up the coast to New York City. A traveler could then continue on to Europe on a through ticket. The first stop on the twenty-day trans-Atlantic voyage would usually be Liverpool, England, from which it would be only a short ferry trip to Ireland, Mollie's birthplace.

The *Panama Star* newspaper of Panama City, Panama, carried the following article in its January 27, 1872, edition: "The steamship *Rising Star* was to have sailed from New York for Aspinwall on 18th inst., touching Jamaica, and will therefore be due here about the 28th instant. The steamer *Alaska* sailed from San Francisco on the 17th inst., and will be due here about the 24th."

The *Alaska* actually sailed from San Francisco two days late, on January 19, 1872, and arrived in Panama City's harbor on February 4. The *Rising Star,* with which the *Alaska* was to connect via the railway, awaited cargo and passengers at Aspinwall. The *Rising Star* departed Aspinwall on February 15, 1872.

The surname "Sheppard" was not particularly common in western America in 1872. At that time, most Irish immigrants landed in New York and remained in the East. One would not normally expect to find the name "Sheppard" on the passenger list of the *Rising Star* steamship. However, the passenger list included the name G. D. Sheppard, a male laborer aged twenty-six traveling in steerage. Is it possible that Ms. Sheppard could have arranged an alteration to the list or disguised herself to travel as a male? Either possibility seems more likely than the coincidence that there was another traveler with the same surname as Mollie from the same clan from Clifton, Ireland.

Or could Mollie Sheppard have taken an alternate means of transportation east, traveling by rail or coach rather than taking the ocean route? This would have been impossible in January 1872 because all rail and coach routes to and from San Francisco were snowbound. Under the headline "The Great Snow Storm: Interruption of Travel on the Railroad—Narrow Escape from Freezing to Death," the *Daily Alta California* reported in mid-December: "It seems that the trains were side-tracked and made secure until efforts could be made to clear the road . . . It is snowing and blowing so that we cannot do a thing, but we are doing all that can be done. It is blowing and drifting here like Sam Hill."

In fact, weather was the reason the *Alaska* was available to carry Ms. Sheppard on her journey. The *Panama Star* carried the following story on February 8, 1872: "The *Alaska*, it will be remembered, was on the line between Aspinwall and New York, but was taken off and sent via the Isthmus of Suez to be put on the line between Japan and San Francisco. She now comes here as an extra steamer, required by the increased freights. The *Alaska* has thus more than circumnavigated the globe since she left New York."

The "increased freights" were the result of the isolation of the West Coast from the East by the heavy snows throughout the Sierra Nevada that winter. Had Mollie intended to travel east by means other than steamship, she would have taken the southern route heading east from Wickenburg rather than west to Los Angeles in late December 1871.

Is it possible that Mollie began her trip home and died at sea, word not reaching William Kruger for many months thereafter? This possibility does not explain the coincidence of a "G. D. Sheppard" on the passenger list of the *Rising Star* steamship. Or, is it possible that Mollie Sheppard's reported death, not reaching publication until May 23, 1874, may have been a ruse to discourage anyone from searching for her and besmirching her reputation in her hometown in Ireland?

In any case, there is no report of Ms. Sheppard's death in California, and her name cannot be found among the cemetery roles of that state. The Daily *Alta California*, diligent in reporting deaths in and around San Francisco, shows no record of Ms. Sheppard's demise during the first half of 1872.

On the other hand, William Kruger, the "sole survivor" of the attack after Mollie's death, found employment in Cleveland, Ohio. It appears that he survived beyond the turn of the century.

Chapter 8

Impregnable Strongholds

Efforts to subjugate the Yavapai tribes continued after the Wickenburg massacre. The Yavapai (or Mojave-Apache Indians) were experts at hiding their rancherias, several of which they considered impregnable. The rare successes experienced by the soldiers in locating Indian encampments only came when a dog barked or a baby cried as the soldiers were about to pass by, often only a few yards away.

General Crook employed Indians to find Indians. Often he found scouts that were enthusiastic about locating and punishing tribes that had warred with them for centuries. One of Crook's trusted scouts was Nantaje or "Joe" to the soldiers. Joe described Nanni-Chaddi's rancheria as nearly impossible to approach, and it was considered impregnable by the Kewevkapaya band of Yavapai who lived there.

In late December 1872 Joe agreed to guide the soldiers to the site. It seemed unlikely that a rancheria existed on the Salt River as described by Joe, because the area had been thoroughly scouted and combed through by troopers for many months. However, Joe had been proven too reliable to dismiss.

The troopers moved by night. They exchanged their boots for moccasins stuffed with straw. All metal accouterments were discarded at the camp site as silence was tantamount. The soldiers, under the command of Maj. William Henry Brown, made their way up the narrow path of loose rocks. Several hundred feet above the canyon floor was a rincon (a sheltered nook) only large enough for a few wickiups and a dozen footsore ponies. Lt. William Ross's detachment was sent ahead to scout and secure the face of the rancheria. A second detachment under Capt. James Burns was ordered to backtrack the trail the ponies had made coming into the rincon.

At the echo of gunfire, Major Brown dispatched Capt. John Bourke, who, with forty troopers, rushed forward to reinforce Lieutenant Ross's detachment. The major followed, cautiously and deliberately, with the remainder of the troopers. The first detachment of soldiers had surprised a band of ninety-four Indians. After a period of ineffective exchanges, Major Brown ordered the troopers to fire at the ceiling of a cave, a shallow clamshell of an indentation with a natural rocky rampart at the face. The shape of the roof ricocheted the bullets into the interior, raining lead projectiles down upon the occupants of the cave.

Captain Burns rushed his detachment toward the sound of the gunfire and found himself on a small mesa above the cave. He rigged harnesses from suspenders, and had two men lean out over the edge to fire down upon the Indians. When the troops expended the bullets in their pistols, they threw the empty guns at the Indians, whereupon Captain Burns decided an alternative strategy was needed. He ordered his men to throw rocks at the Indians and start rock slides wherever the ground was crumbling. The combined assault from above and below resulted in the deaths of seventy-six men, women, and children, and the capture of eighteen more.

The camps of Chuntz and Delt-che were on the opposite side of the mountain, so they came too late to help. The chiefs of those camps then decided to move their people, three hundred to four hundred Indians, to Turret Butte—their last impenetrable rancheria. En route the Indians encountered three white men: John MacDonald, A. C. "Gus" Swain, and George Taylor. The *Weekly Arizona Miner* reported on March 15, 1873:

Another Horrid Butchery of White Men by Apaches

A. C. Swain, well and favorably known here for ten years past, and a man named John MacDonald, were on the afternoon of the 11th Inst. attacked and murdered by Apaches near the sink of the Hassayampa (River), some 13 miles below the town of Wickenburg in this county. Of these horrid deeds we have been aprised [sic] by Mr. Brennan, driver of Grant's stage, by a letter from H. Mannasse of Wickenburg and the following letter from C. G. Terry to H. Partridge of this place.

Wickenburg, March 12, 1873

It is my painful duty to impart to you that yesterday A. C. Swain, and a man whose name is unknown, was murdered by Indians at a point twelve miles below here, on the road between here and Phoenix. The circumstances as far as I can get information were as follows: On Tuesday, Swain left home for the purpose of taking water and provisions to some men in his employ at or in the vicinity of Nigger Wells. On his return, as is shown by apparent indentations on the battleground, he was overtaken by 300 or 400 Indians who were coming from East to West and are supposed to be going to some reservations (perhaps Date Creek) and there killed in company with the other man. When found the bodies were stripped of their clothing, their weapons taken, also a horse and mule that Swain was driving. And from appearances the mule was killed and eaten by them (the Indians) at the place aforementioned. Gus was aired with seven arrows, three of which were yet in his body, his skull was mashed in with rocks, in fact his body was horribly mutilated. The body of MacDonald was found about ten yards from the place of the attack partially covered up in the sand and five or six arrows in his breast, his head also mashed in

113

with rocks. As the man who saw the arrows, (George) Monroe said he was confident they were Apache-Mohaves.

Two old men had found Swain and MacDonald the morning after they were murdered, while the old-timers were out looking for stock they had lost during the morning hours. They prepared to bury the men when one noticed the markings in the sand where the Indians had dragged young Taylor. They followed the trail, and when they came to a clearing these hardened frontiersmen averted their eyes at first sight of the body. The manner of finally killing George Taylor, after he had become poor sport, was so horrible that they could not look at him directly. They reluctantly told their story once, but then Capt. Azor H. Nickerson demanded that they retell it. Still disbelieving them, the captain went to examine the site and to exhume the remains of young Taylor for further examination. Nickerson reported, "no less than one hundred and fifty of these cruel missiles had broken off in his body. They finished him in a manner so excruciating and beastly that I cannot even hint at the method of his final taking off."

The description of 150 missiles suggests that the manner of the game was to take splinters, probably about half an arrow shaft whittled to needle sharpness, and to stab them with surgical precision into young Taylor by hand, careful not to kill their victim. No other method could have prolonged his agony throughout such a lengthy ordeal. It was suggested that some splinters had been set aflame, perhaps when young Taylor's response to the pain had dulled. The manner of Taylor's "taking off" cannot even be suggested considering the horrible manner of torture often described in exquisite detail in the literature, yet here no description is given because it was "too excruciating and beastly."

Within twenty-four hours the army had mobilized First Lt. Max Wesendorff of the 1st Cavalry, First Lt. Albert E. Woodson of the 5th

Cavalry, First Lt. Edwin A. Rice of the 23rd Infantry, and Capt. George M. Randall of the 23rd Infantry. These detachments took up the pursuit. Several of them had luck in finding and killing hostile Indians, but none of these Indians were the perpetrators of what had then become known as the "Taylor massacre." It was Captain Randall and his troopers who finally ran them to ground.

Captain Randall led Company 1 of the 23rd Infantry and Company A of the Indian Scouts under Chief of Scouts Corydon Eliphalet Cooley with Sergeant of Scouts Alchise. Company 1 and Company A left Fort McDowell and cut a week-old trace shortly after leaving the fort. It was leading in the direction they were already traveling, so they followed it. Soon the trace was crossed by a newer trail, heading across rough country along the edge of the Bradshaw Mountains. Alchise advised Randall that these Indians were going to their second impregnable stronghold at Turret Butte, high ground from which the Indians could see for miles in any direction. Alchise described the method by which he could take Company A into the stronghold. He said he would march scouts to within ten miles of the Butte. They would then crawl on hands and knees for several miles. Finally, the scouts would continue on their stomachs until they came to and surrounded the rancheria. All this, the Indian scout warned, must be done in complete silence and before dawn. Against objections by Cooley, Captain Randall approved the plan but ordered the scouts to lead the troopers into the stronghold.

As the two companies neared the mountain peak, the trail freshened. They arrived at the campsite before dusk and settled in. Randall ordered his men to wrap their booted feet and knees with gunny sacks to quiet them and to protect them from the mal pais, or volcanic rock. As soon as the sun set they began the long, arduous journey. The ground was rough with lava beds that were difficult to crawl over and there were small cracks and crevices to maneuver.

The Apache scouts stayed out in front. If anything looked suspicious they would signal the soldiers to stop and lay still. They would then reconnoiter the area before moving on.

The two companies crawled and dragged themselves for ten miles. The last two miles were up the side of the mountain. When they reached the top, they worked their way around the peak until they finally came upon a flat area of about two acres at the highest point. There the rancheria was situated. The Indians were so confident of their impregnability that they had posted no guards. It was still an hour before dawn, so the company of soldiers and scouts quietly surrounded the rancheria on two sides—the other two sides were sheer cliffs.

At dawn the Indians began to stir. Immediately, the army troopers and scouts opened a rapid volley of fire. The Indians were so startled that many ran past rocks and weapons and jumped over the side of the sheer cliff. Most worked their way down the escarpment. More than half of the Indians managed to escape.

Property found at the rancheria confirmed that these were the Indians responsible for the killings of the three white men south of Wickenburg. Alchise provided Captain Randall with property belonging to Taylor, Swain, and MacDonald and reported that 47 hostile Indians were dead and 136 were taken prisoner.

The next few weeks passed quietly, and were marked by the absence of Indian trouble. Finally, a delegation of Yavapai Indians approached the command at Camp Verde to announce that their chief wanted to come and speak of peace. On April 6, 1873, Chief Cha-lipun came to Camp Verde with three hundred Indians. "I represent ten times this many," he told General Crook. He continued:

> We are not here because we love you, Nantan Lupan,
> but because we fear you. We have never been afraid of the

Whites or the Mexicans, but now our own people fight against us. You have too many cartridges of copper and we cannot go to sleep at night because we are afraid that we will be surrounded by the walk-a-heap soldiers before daybreak. We cannot hunt because the noise of our guns will attract the yellowlegs. We cannot cook mescal or anything else because the flames and smoke would draw down the soldiers. We cannot live in the valley because there are too many soldiers, so we have retreated to the mountain tops to hide in the snow, but the scouts find us and the soldiers follow them.

General Crook took the chief's hand and held it. The humbling of this once great Indian was evident to every man present. Crook explained:

Not one Apache has been killed except by his own folly. He refused to listen to the messengers we sent out to tell him to come in to the reservation. There is no use trying to say who started the war, because there are bad men in both camps, white and Indian, but now we must sue for peace. There are things that you must do. You must wear tags to identify you so long as there are bad Indians off the reservation and you must stop cutting the noses off your wives when you are jealous of them. You must stop killing and I will be the best friend you ever had. You must make this peace, not for a day or a week, but for all time.

As a result of the meeting, a reservation of eight hundred square miles was established "forever and forever." It consisted of fertile, forested lands along both sides of a river at a high altitude where it was cool and game was plentiful.

Chapter 9

Removal, Relocation, and Concentration

There was a monstrous tug of war going on between political forces in Arizona during the early 1870s. Business-minded contractors in Prescott fought to retain the fifteen hundred Yavapais and Tonto-Apache Indians living at Camp Verde as the contracts to supply their needs were lucrative. The infamous "Tucson Ring" (the influential men who exploited the Indian supply processes) had the support of the greater number of politicians, so bureaucrats fought equally hard to have the Indians transferred to the San Carlos Agency. In the balance were the contracts that could make a man rich in a very short period of time and give him the opportunity to run his business from such places as El Paso, Santa Fe, or San Francisco, or he could sell out and retire.

The Tucson Ring had the support of Prescott's farmers. The farmers around Prescott had begun to look with envy at the fertile land that the Indians had cultivated with great success for several years, and so they supported the relocation.

In 1874 the Indians once again had prepared the land for planting, but the promised seeds did not arrive. Tribal spokesperson Pakakiva suggested, "Somebody make bad medicine." The bad medicine he referred to was the Indians' pending removal and relocation as a part of the first real test of the government's Indian policy in the Southwest.

At their first meeting in Prescott, General Crook told Levi

Dudley, Superintendent of Indian Affairs in New Mexico, that he would give him all the support and cooperation he could, short of using military force. Dudley was confidant he could manipulate the Indians into cooperating with their relocation. Dudley's reception at Camp Verde was mixed. Most people here opposed to the move, and few believed it could be done. Dudley was arrogant and patronizing as he told the Indians that he had come on behalf of President Ulysses S. Grant in Washington with orders to move them from their homes to another place.

The Indians had been restless and suspicious ever since Deltche, who had "broken out" in a peaceful escape, had snuck back onto the reservation with predictions that they would lose their homelands. Sergeant Chief Snook, one of Al Sieber's scouts, spoke for the Indians: "We will not go where we will be outnumbered by our enemies. This is our country and always has been. Our fathers, our grandfathers, our wives and children have all been born here where our ancestors have died. Your General Grant has made promises that the country for forty miles along the river and ten miles on either side should be ours forever."

After the meeting with Dudley, a small group of Indians approached Doctor William H. Corbusier[42] to learn more about Dudley and his orders to move them. Corbusier confirmed that the order had come from President Grant. When pressed, he agreed that he would accompany them on their journey. Only then did the Indians agree to go quietly. The doctor strongly recommended that the tribes be taken by wagon road around the mountains. He stressed to Dudley that the Indians would cooperate, but not cheerfully. The doctor knew that the best way for him to help the Indians was to ensure that the move went as smoothly as possible, and being at odds with the president's representative would not help matters. Dudley, however, responded that he had moved Indians before and that the Indians were familiar with travel over rough country, especially mountains.

It took three days to gather the Indians and move them from the reservation to Camp Verde. General Crook had provided a pack train with twenty-nine mules and a cavalry escort of fifteen troopers led by Lt. George O. Eaton.[43] The general gave instructions, but left his advice short of official orders. He told Lieutenant Eaton that if the Indians wanted to fight among themselves he should let them. But, if it came to a point where government property or the safety of the command were endangered, the lieutenant must stop them.

Dudley had supplemented the general's pack train with another one consisting of twenty-six mules. Even so, it was evident that there would not be enough food for a trip of 180 miles. He immediately distributed the flour from his pack train and sent the empty pack train to Fort McDowell to requisition another five thousand pounds of food. Dudley directed his packers to meet the party halfway down the trail.

The Indians were familiar with the terrain they would cross—the high mountains with storm-swollen streams and rivers. They had to carry all their belongings on their backs. None had adequate clothing, and many were barefoot. One ancient warrior, concerned that his feeble wife could not survive the long walk, cut leg holes in a basket for her to ride, lifted her onto his back, supported the load with a tumpline across his forehead, and carried her the entire distance. Some Yavapais simply refused to go. Instead they went to Rattlesnake Cañon and Hell Cañon to live in their traditional way, hunting and gathering food. There was no time or men to pursue them so they were left behind to be dealt with later.

Al Sieber[44] looked over the 1,426 Indians assembled for the trip, half Tonto-Apache and the other half a mix of Yavapais and Hualapais. Sieber had the Tontos take the lead, which they greatly disliked. The Tontos did not like having enemies of centuries at their backs, and Sieber sensed that the tribes needed to be separated on the trail or trouble would surely follow.

Dudley, already nicknamed "come-along" for his constant prod-
ding, left for Prescott as the Indians left Camp Verde. From Prescott
he wired John Clum to meet them north of the San Carlos agency
with more food. He caught up with the group on the second day. The
Indian travelers were already sullen and discouraged by the severe
snowstorm that had greeted them on their first day on the trail. They
would have to make better than five miles a day if they were to reach
the San Carlos Reservation safely. Medicine men saw evil omens
everywhere and chanted continuously. Soon the chanting was
drowned out by the wailing of hungry, tired women and children.

Each day the Tontos increased the gap between themselves and
the Yavapais and Hualapais. Sieber was concerned that they would
soon outdistance the column and break away. But each night the
Tontos set up their camp and came in for food and supplies. Twice a
deer was killed along the way. The meat was intended to be shared
by all the hungry Indians, but the Tontos were in the lead and took
it all. After the second incident, the children of the Yavapais and
Hualapais began taunting the Tontos in their camp. Then the adults
joined in on both sides. One Yavapai woman yelled out, "Kill the
Tontos," and a wild volley of gunfire erupted.

Soldiers and Al Sieber sprinted up the hill, positioning themselves between the two warring factions. Sieber yelled over the
sound of gunfire to stop, and glared at each side. The firing ceased
immediately, since there were no enemy targets visible on either
side and there was no point in wasting precious ammunition. Only
the quick actions of Sieber and the troopers prevented a massacre.
Several chiefs from each faction were then brought together and
forced to agree that they would not fight on the trail. "The weather
and terrain are enemy enough," Sieber argued, and they all had to
agree.

Spring rains had not yet made the streams and rivers impassa-
ble, but they were swollen and the water was icy cold. Each time

they came to a crossing it took a long time to get the people, animals, and supplies across. Eaton, adamant that he would not subject these souls to the freezing water, had the troopers shuttle the old women and children across on their horses. It took an entire night to cross the first large river they came upon, and then they rested an entire day afterwards.

By the time the supplemental shipment of flour arrived from Fort McDowell, everyone was hungry. Many of the cattle and other animals had become footsore and had to be left behind. The Indians were becoming quite restless by the time they came to the Salt River. Dudley insisted that they couldn't spend two days at every river crossing. He ordered that the Indians wade across. Eaton agreed that they couldn't chance another long delay, with the food supplies diminishing so rapidly, so he had his troopers help the children and elderly across. The rest had to wade through the icy waters.

Dudley had sent the message to Clum requesting that he meet the party with food, but he knew that the telegraph wires didn't go directly to the agency and couldn't be sure Clum received his telegram. He sensed murderous hostility against him for the hardships everyone had suffered. Several Yavapais and Hualapais had painted their faces black and their noses red, as if preparing for war. When they appeared near his tent in war paint, Dudley quickly agreed to ride ahead to look for the food shipment. Dudley had ridden out of camp only a mile when he encountered twenty-five cattle and mules being watered at a spring. The drovers had brought a half ton of flour. Dudley returned to his camp with the good news and moved the Indians that one extra mile to better water and food. Now fed and rested the party moved on to their new home, only thirty-five miles further south.

A few older Indians died on the trip. Additionally, eight men had died in the skirmish between the hostile bands, but two babies had also been born on the trail. More than seventy Indians had fled

to the Colorado River Reservation or north to join their clans in the
cañons around Camp Verde, but 1,321 tired Indians walked onto the
San Carlos Reservation in darkness.

At sunrise the Indians had their first look at their new home.
San Carlos was a desolate, barren place. Being winter, the new
arrivals could not imagine the unbearable heat and swarms of malar-
ial mosquitoes that awaited them in a few months. The rancherias
consisted of familiar wickiups covered with brush, grass, old blankets, or deerskins. The settlements smelled of smoke, garbage, and
human waste. Lean, mangy dogs lay about or fought with one
another over some discarded morsel of food. The agency buildings
were low adobe walls with mud-plastered grass roofs. There was no
way to compare this desolate place with the freshness of their mountain reservation of fertile farmlands and forests. All the "bad medicine," all the wrongs of the past fifty years, seemed to be revisited
upon the Indians at San Carlos in their new home.

John Philip Clum, the agent in charge at the San Carlos reservation, came early to talk with them. He was a young man, short and
balding, with a walrus moustache. They would learn that he was a
charismatic and stubborn leader. Most important, however, he was
fair and had a genuine concern for his wards. Clum had established
a policy that prohibited Indians on the reservation from being
armed, except for those few selected as agency policemen. He tried
to coax the weapons from the new arrivals, but they panicked at the
thought of being among their enemies unarmed.

The Tontos, Yavapais, and Hualapais, enemies for centuries,
united in common defense of Clum's order. They gathered their few
possessions and hurried across the river where they camped in sight
of the agency. They were afraid to return and lose their guns, but
hesitant to flee further because they feared army reprisals.

Two days passed before Clum sent an emissary to tell the
Indians that food ration tickets would be exchanged for guns. The

hungry Indians finally made a token gesture by sending seventy-five of their oldest, most worn weapons and exchanged them for food. Finally, Clum negotiated the surrender of the remainder of their guns and ammunition, and appointed several men from each tribe as agency policemen.

Guns were still available to the Indians, however, for hunting. Clum issued passes to the Indians who would hunt in the surrounding countryside and issued weapons and ammunition to those selected to provide meat for their tribe. Even though they kept good faith and turned in their guns after each hunt, armed Indians outside the reservation continued to cause concern. If an Indian left the reservation without a pass, or if he had a pass but was not in the prescribed area, he was killed by soldiers. Many Anglos remained so fearful of the Indians that they opened fire without first inquiring about a pass, but if the Indians retaliated their punishment was swift and severe.

Camp Verde was the first major test of the government's removal, relocation, and concentration policy in the Southwest. The Indians who were moved from their reservation north of Prescott to the San Carlos Reservation were to be there for the next quarter century. The application of the government's policy to the Yavapai Indians was not the result of the Wickenburg massacre. However, it is difficult to imagine that this tribe, which was in 1874 being cooperative and capable of supporting themselves, could have been subjected to the new government policy had it not been for the change in eastern attitudes resulting from the massacre.

1. Royal Emerson Whitman was born in Maine in 1833. Whitman, who arrived in Arizona in November 1870, became one of the most reviled men in the territory. Whitman died in Washington, D.C., on February 12, 1913.

2. Prescott, Arizona Territory, the only U.S. territorial capital founded in a wilderness, grew up around gold mines discovered by the Walker party in 1863. Prescott later became central Arizona's hub for trading and freighting. In 1891 Captain John Bourke wrote in *On the Border with Crook*:

> Prescott was not merely picturesque in location and dainty in appearance, with all its houses neatly painted and surrounded with paling fences and supplied with windows after the American style—it was a village transplanted bodily from the centre of the Delaware, the Mohawk, or the Connecticut valley. Everything about the houses recalled the scenes familiar to the dweller in the country near Pittsburg or other busy community. The houses were built with American bolts and locks, opened by American knobs, and not closed by letting a heavy cottonwood log fall against them.
>
> The furniture was the neat cottage furniture with which all must be familiar who have ever had the privilege of entering an American country home; there were carpets, mirrors, rocking-chairs, tables, lamps, and all other appurtenances, just as one might expect to find

them in any part of the country excepting Arizona and
New Mexico.

3. The Arizona Stagecoach Company, established in 1865 as the Arizona Consolidated Stage and Livery Company, carried U.S. Mail, express, and passengers from San Bernardino, California, to Prescott, Arizona Territory. The main station, corrals, and repair station were located at Wickenburg in November 1871.

4. Wickenburg, Arizona Territory, was founded near the Hassayampa River to support the miners at the Vulture Mine a few miles west. In 1864 it was a camp consisting of a few tents, but later these were replaced by adobe dwellings. In 1865 a post office was established. Two years later the town had grown to two hundred inhabitants, all dependent on the Vulture Mine for their livelihood.

5. George Montague Wheeler was born at Hopkinton, Massachusetts, on October 9, 1842. He was commissioned second lieutenant of engineers on June 18, 1866; he became a first lieutenant on March 7, 1867 and was promoted to captain on March 4, 1879. Lieutenant Wheeler surveyed and mapped the West between 1871 and 1888. He retired June 15, 1888. By act of the U.S. Congress in 1890, Captain Wheeler was promoted to the rank of major retroactive to July 23, 1888. After retirement he lived in New York City, where he died on May 3, 1905.

6. Ehrenberg, Arizona Territory, formerly Bradshaw's Ferry, was founded in 1868 when the Colorado River changed its course, leaving dry the town of La Paz five miles to the north.

7. "Dutch" John Lance was one of the best long-distance drivers on the frontier. He had recently secured employment with the Arizona Stage Company and was making his first return trip to Ehrenberg when he was killed by Indians eight miles west of Wickenburg on November 5, 1871. His name has often been misspelled in literature as Lantz, Lanz, Lentz, Lenz, and others.

8. Culling's Well, dug by Englishman Charles C. Culling, was nearly three hundred feet deep to ensure "a never ending flow of pure sweet water." It was the only stable source of water between Wickenburg and Ehrenberg. Also known as the "Lighthouse of the Desert," it was located along the Centennial Wash thirty-six miles west of Wickenburg. Culling died in 1878 and his widow married John Drew, who managed the well until it outlived its usefulness.

9. La Paz seemed to spring up overnight in 1862 when Pauline Weaver and others discovered gold placers along the Colorado River above Fort Yuma. The town was situated on the east bank of the river and by the end of 1862 its population had increased to several hundred inhabitants with several stores, a bakery, and a feed corral.

10. The *Miner* newspaper was purchased in 1867 by John Huguenot Marion, who published the paper until 1877. Marion died in Prescott on July 27, 1891.

11. James O. Grant arrived in San Francisco from Canada in June 1852. Initially he was in the mercantile business but later owned the pony express from Los Angeles to Prescott. Grant established the Arizona Consolidated Stage and Livery Company, which later became the Arizona Stage Company. Grant died of exhaustion in San Bernardino in May 1875 after searching for a shorter route west. He was fifty-four years old at the time of his death. In 1874 Grant took on J. J. Valentine as a partner. Valentine continued to run the company after Grant's death.

12. Camp Date Creek was first established as a temporary camp at Dobbins Ranch in 1865 and abandoned on October 12, 1866. Dobbins's Ranch later came into the possession of William Gilson. On May 11, 1867, another military camp was established three miles east of the previous location on the south bank of Date Creek, and in November 1868 it was renamed Camp Date Creek.

The new camp was built around a parade ground with two enlisted men's barracks, kitchen, and post bake house on the north; four sets of officer's quarters on the south; tent guard houses on the east; and the hospital on the west. The barracks, constructed of adobe, had peaked shingle roofs. The officer's quarters, also of adobe, were single rooms measuring twenty-six feet by thirteen feet with earthen roofs.

Outside the main compound and to the east was the laundress's quarters and to the south was the storeroom. Looking north were the herders tents and haystacks and just beyond them the corrals. The far northwest corner included the blacksmith's and carpenter's shops and the quartermaster commissary store.

In the early 1870s Yavapai (Apache-Mojave) Indians began settling near the camp, and the area became a temporary reservation. In June 1873 the Indians were moved to the Rio Verde Reservation and Camp Date Creek was ordered abandoned in September 1873.

13. Abbot and Downing Company began in 1813 when Lewis Downing opened a wheelwright shop in Concord, New Hampshire, and in 1816 built a small factory there. One of the men he hired was J. Stephens Abbot, who became his partner in 1828. Downing's father had been a stagecoach driver who encouraged him to design a stagecoach that, unlike English coaches, would not be top heavy and prone to tip over on the rough American roads. The coach he designed—the Concord—became the standard for American stagecoaches.

14. W. H. Ball ran a profitable freighting business from Wilmington, California, to Prescott and Phoenix until the railroad put him out of business in 1884. Ball died in Anaheim, California, in 1895.

15. Frederick Henry Ernst Ebstein was born April 21, 1847, in Prussia, but by 1861 his family had moved to Poughkeepsie, New York. Ebstein enlisted November 18, 1864, and was com-

missioned a lieutenant on September 12, 1867. He was assigned, with wife Jeannie, to Camp Date Creek on September 28, 1869. The Ebsteins remained at Camp Date Creek until August 6, 1872. He was promoted to captain April 1, 1885, to major January 16, 1899, and retired July 8, 1899. He died on February 8, 1916, in Brooklyn, New York.

16. Charles Meinhold was born in Berlin, Germany, in 1827. He enlisted in Philadelphia on May 5, 1851, at which time he described himself as five feet nine and a half inches tall with hazel eyes and dark hair. He was promoted to captain on December 1, 1866; began service with Company B, 3rd Cavalry at Camp McDowell, Arizona Territory, on March 19, 1870; and moved to Camp Date Creek in August 1871. In December 1871 his company was reassigned to Nebraska. He died December 14, 1877, in Clifton Springs, New York.

17. James Ferdinand Simpson was born at Hingham, Massachusetts, on October 25, 1841. He was appointed second lieutenant on August 17, 1867, and transferred to the 3rd Cavalry on March 15, 1871. He retired November 25, 1887, and died in Prescott, Arizona, on June 29, 1899.

18. Richard Fitzgerald O'Beirne was born in Canada on October 21, 1833. He was appointed lieutenant on May 14, 1861; captain on October 25, 1861; and assumed command of Camp Date Creek in August 1869, where he remained until August 6, 1872. O'Bierne was promoted to major on March 20, 1879; lieutenant colonel on April 18, 1884; and colonel on January 31, 1891. He died less than a month after his last promotion on February 24, 1891.

19. Joseph Lawson was born in Ireland in 1821. He served during the Civil War, then was commissioned second lieutenant in the 3rd Cavalry in 1866. He was promoted to first lieutenant on July 28, 1866. He joined Company B at Camp Date Creek on

November 24, 1870, where he remained until December 1871. He was promoted to captain on September 25, 1876. He died at Fort Fred Steele on January 30, 1881.

20. George Crook was born on September 8, 1828, near Taylorsville, Ohio. He graduated from West Point in 1852 and served on the western frontier until the outbreak of the Civil War. He returned west in 1866. Crook assumed command of the Department of Arizona on June 4, 1871, and arrived at Tucson on June 19; he was promoted to brigadier general on October 29, 1873, and relinquished his Arizona command on March 22, 1875. He was promoted to major general on April 6, 1888, and died in Chicago, Illinois, on March 21, 1890.

21. Charles Baldwin Genung was born at Penn Yan, Yaters County, New York, on July 22, 1839. He moved to California in 1855 and then, due to illness, moved to Arizona in 1863 where he became a successful prospector, rancher, farmer, and family man. Genung died on August 16, 1916, at his home in Peeples Valley and was buried at Prescott, Arizona.

22. Ocho-cama was shot at twice and pierced once with a bayonet while escaping from the Date Creek guardhouse on September 8, 1872. An Apache-Yuma Indian reported that Ocho-cama had died of his wounds within a few days, but a week later Crook learned that Ocho-cama was alive and plotting to attack the Colorado River Indian Reservation to kill Chief Irataba. Ocho-cama survived the attack at Burro Creek on September 28, 1872, and was involved in the move to San Carlos in February 1875.

23. John Gregory Bourke was born in Philadelphia on June 23, 1846. He served in the Civil War and then attended West Point, graduating in 1869. He moved to Arizona from his station in New Mexico and from mid-1871 served as aide to Gen. George Crook for the next fifteen years. Bourke was promoted to first lieutenant May 17, 1876, and to captain on June 26, 1882.

During the last thirty years of his life he became an accomplished author and Indian ethnologist. Bourke died in Philadelphia, Pennsylvania, on June 8, 1896.

24. George Monroe was born at Floyd County, Indiana, in 1835. He arrived in the Arizona Territory on May 21, 1862, and served three years as a private in the 1st California Infantry, which was credited with saving the territories for the union.

   Monroe was one of Arizona's "most ancient Hassayampers," spending his entire adult life in or about Wickenburg. He is credited with the discovery of Castle Creek Hot Springs. In early 1864 Monroe listed his occupation as soldier, but he mustered out at Fort Whipple later that year and became a miner. He had a number of successes mining gold and in 1883 had a fine lead mine near Wickenburg. By 1888 Monroe was again mining gold at his King Solomon mine.

   George Monroe led the pursuit posse the day following the Wickenburg massacre. He and his four posse men were the first on the scene to conduct an investigation and concluded, beyond a doubt, that the Indians at the Date Creek Reservation had committed the crime. Monroe died in Wickenburg on December 28, 1897, from a bout of pneumonia.

25. Dan O'Leary was born in Ireland about 1834. He was one of Arizona's best-known guides and army scouts. Along with Lieutenant Ross, he was one of the two men responsible for saving General Crook's life on September 8, 1872. O'Leary died at Needles, California, in 1900.

26. William Gilson was born at Leinster, Ireland, in 1834. He arrived in La Paz on October 14, 1863, and mined the Walnut Grove area until he purchased Robbins Ranch, site of the original Camp Date Creek. Gilson was one of the first to raise stock and farm carp in Skull Valley. He sold his ranch in 1883 and moved to Phoenix.

Gilson's sister was the laundress at Camp Date Creek when Mollie Sheppard was brought in for medical treatment. Ms. Sheppard was put up at the laundress' quarters until she was well enough to be removed from the military post to continue her recuperation at the Gilson ranch.

Gilson was a supporter of the Indians at Camp Date Creek. Still, he gave testimony which helped convince General Crook that the perpetrators of the Wickenburg massacre were Camp Date Creek Indians.

William Gilson died near Phoenix on January 31, 1909.

27. George Hall Burton was born January 12, 1843, in Delaware. He was commissioned lieutenant on June 23, 1865, and promoted to captain August 16, 1871. In January 1872 he took a detachment to the Colorado River Indian Reservation to protect the agent, suppress disturbances, and investigate the Wickenburg stagecoach massacre.

Burton moved through the ranks to brigadier general effective April 12, 1903, and retired in September 1906. He died in Los Angeles, California, on October 20, 1917.

28. Colorado River Indian Reservation was set aside for the Mohave Indians in 1865.

29. Irataba was a chief of the Mohave Indians at the Colorado River Indian Reservation. He was a tall, large man of a quiet, observant, and thoughtful demeanor. He remained a friend of the Whites throughout his life, though his friendship was sorely tested on several occasions. He died on May 3, 1874, near the banks of the Colorado River.

30. John Alexis Tonner was born July 21, 1841, at Wilmington, Delaware. He received his appointment as Indian agent for the Colorado River Indian Reservation on July 13, 1871. He wanted the position of superintendent but, on the day Herman Bendell resigned, that position was abolished by executive order.

31. Herman Bendell, born in Albany, New York, on October 28, 1843, became superintendent of Indian affairs in the Arizona Territory from March 1871 through June 1873. He died in Albany, New York, on November 14, 1932.

32. Oliver Otis Howard (Gen.) was born November 8, 1830, in Leeds, Maine. He graduated from West Point in 1854. He died at his Vermont home on October 26, 1909.

33. Frank E. Hill, a private, was stabbed during the Date Creek incident of September 8, 1872. His wounds were at first thought fatal. He survived and on August 12, 1875, Sgt. Frank E. Hill was awarded the Medal of Honor for his actions that day with the citation, "Secured the person of a hostile Apache Chief, although while holding the chief he was severely wounded in the back by another Indian."

34. John Philip Clum was born in New York State on September 1, 1851. As a member of the Dutch Reform Church he was assigned to supervise the Apaches at the San Carlos Reservation, where he remained from February 1874 until July 1877. Clum became a prominent newspaper man throughout the Arizona Territory until 1882. He died at Los Angeles, California, on May 2, 1932.

35. Julius Wilmot Mason was born in Pennsylvania in 1837. He was an engineer when the Civil War broke out and was appointed a second lieutenant in the Cavalry. Mason arrived in Arizona in February 1872. During the next decade he suffered several bouts of debilitating disease before contracting apoplexy, the disease that killed him at Fort Huachuca on December 19, 1882.

36. Fort Whipple was first established in Chino Valley but moved to Granite Creek about a mile northeast of Prescott on May 18, 1864. The fort became headquarters for General Crook in mid-1871.

37. Jeannie Virginia Smith Ebstein married Lt. F. H. E. Ebstein on February 2, 1869, in Brooklyn, New York. When Mollie Sheppard

was taken to Camp Date Creek for medical attention, Jeannie, the only officer's wife present, offered her clothing, a truly compassionate act considering Mollie's status of "soiled dove."

38. Endorsements of the army upon Gilson's request explain as follows:

Date Creek Camp

Commd'g Officer

(J. 1, 1872)

Endorsements on letter from William Gilson dated Camp Date Creek Reservation, December 15, 1871, states that he is living on a tract of 160 acres of land claimed to be within the Mail Reservation of Camp Date Creek which he bought in 1867 from a person who had occupied it since 1865; that he was obliged in 1871 to take a lease of the same from the Government. Represents that he is prevented from entering this land so as to secure a title and requests that action be taken so that he may be placed in control of the same.

1st ENDORSEMENT

Returned to C.O. Camp Date Creek for information and report Jan. 4, 1872.

2nd ENDORSEMENT

Headquarters Camp Date Creek, A.T.

January 16, 1872

Respectfully returned. I have no certain means of learning how long the land referred to herein has been in the occupancy of Mr. Gilson. I am informed that it was the site of a military post in 1865, and that a portion of the buildings now occupied by Mr. Gilson were constructed by United States troops, that subsequently the place was abandoned and the land occupied by the parties from whom Mr. Gilson purchased. Mr. Gilson has occupied the land since February 14, 1865, through permission of the military authorities. In compliance with G. O. No. 74 (A. G. O. of 1869) and instruction from the Department Commander the land was leased to him on 1st January, 1871, for the nominal sum of one dollar.

As nearly all the wood suitable for fuel now on this reserve is on the land in question and as the great scarcity of fuel in this vicinity is a subject mostly of consideration and also that for the proper protection of discipline so far as guarding against the selling and bartering of liquor to the troops of this post is concerned—that the ranch occupied by Mr. Gilson should be in control of the military authorities, I would respectfully recommend it be leased to him under the same instructions as that of last year.

The original lease is forwarded for the information of the Department Commander.

Signed: O'Bierne
Captain, 21st Infantry
Commanding Post

3rd ENDORSEMENT

Headquarters Department of Arizona
Prescott, January 27, 1872

Respectfully returned to Mr. Gilson via Commanding Officer Camp Date Creek.

This portion of the reserve being necessary for the public service, it cannot be released to Mr. Gilson for the present.

So long as there is no reasonable ground for complaint against him he is authorized to occupy, under the present arrangements the ranch, so that when it is abandoned by the Government he can perfect his title.

George Crook

Lt. Colonel, 23rd Infantry

Brevet Major General, Commanding

39. David Jones (Dr.) Evans was the post physician at Camp Date Creek in November 1871. He provided medical attention for William Kruger and Mollie Sheppard at the post and later at William Gilson's Ranch before he concluded his contract with the army in 1872. Dr. Evans continued his practice in San Bernardino, California, where he died of a lingering illness on March 8, 1896.

40. The telegraph into the Arizona Territory was established on November 18, 1873, with the first line running from department headquarters at Fort Whipple to existing facilities in San Diego. The line was extended to Fort Lowell and Tucson, by December and ultimately connected all posts to Fort Whipple.

41. Frederick Kruger was William Kruger's brother, and, as a civilian employee of the army, was also reassigned to Ehrenberg. However, Frederick did not travel with his brother on that fateful stagecoach ride. He remained behind to complete his duties at the quartermaster's office at Fort Whipple and to sell his mining claims in the Tiger and Pine Grove Districts. He advertised the sale of those claims in the *Miner* on October 21, 1871.

42. Dr. William Corbusier was born in New York City on April 10, 1844. He graduated from Bellevue Hospital Medical College on March 1, 1867, and soon after served as army surgeon at Camp Verde. He retired several times, finally as a colonel on August 15, 1919. He died on February 7, 1930, at San Francisco, California.

43. George O. Eaton was born in Maine on May 14, 1848. He enlisted in 1865 and was appointed to West Point in 1869. He arrived in the Arizona Territory in December 1873. He resigned

his commission on March 29, 1883. Eaton died at Fort Myers, Florida, on September 12, 1930.

44. Albert Sieber was born at Bad Mingolsheim, Germany, on February 29, 1844. Sieber became the best known army scout serving in the Arizona Territory. He was killed on February 19, 1907, at the Tonto Storage Reservoir when a boulder of five tons or more rolled over him.

November 4, 1871

6:53 a.m.	Sunrise.
7:00 a.m.	Stagecoach leaves Prescott.
5:36 p.m.	Sunset.
6:02 p.m.	End civil twilight.
8:00 p.m.	Fifty Indians leave Date Creek Reservation.
11:25 p.m.	Moonrise (last quarter, waning).
12:00 a.m.	Stagecoach arrives at Wickenburg.

November 5, 1871

4:00 a.m.	Thirty Indians arrive at the attack site and prepare for the ambush. Ball's teamsters begin the morning drive toward Wickenburg.
6:28 a.m.	Civil twilight.
6:54 a.m.	Sunrise.
7:00 a.m.	Stagecoach leaves Wickenburg.
7:15 a.m.	John Nelson, mail carrier, leaves Culling's Well eastbound for Wickenburg.
7:20 a.m.	Aaron Barnett dismounts stagecoach and returns to Wickenburg.
8:00 a.m.	"Dutch" John Lance sounds alarm, "Apaches . . . " First volley fired—Lance is killed. Seconds later a second volley is fired—Shoholm is dead from the

volleys. Ball's teamsters are eight miles west of attack scene, sixteen miles west of Wickenburg.

8:04 a.m.   P. M. Hamel exits coach.

8:06 a.m.   W. G. Salmon exits coach.

8:08 a.m.   W. G. Salmon killed.

8:11 a.m.   P. M. Hamel killed as William Kruger and Mollie Sheppard make good their escape from the stagecoach.

8:12 a.m.   Nine Indians go in pursuit of Kruger and Sheppard. The escaping pair stays away from the roadway to seek cover, slowed by soft sand.

9:20 a.m.   Ball's teamsters pass Kruger and Sheppard, neither aware of the other, four miles west of the stagecoach.

9:45 a.m.   Kruger and Sheppard retake the roadway, note freighter's wagon tracks. Pursuing Indians also note tracks and rush back to stagecoach to warn other Indians.

10:00 a.m. Kruger and Sheppard stop John Nelson, convince him to take them to Cullings Well.

11:00 a.m. Indians set stagecoach on fire, depart scene of the attack.

12:00 p.m. Teamsters arrive at stagecoach.

1:00 p.m.   Nelson, Kruger, and Sheppard arrive at Culling's Well.

1:30 p.m.   Teamsters head north to Date Creek army post; Nelson heads south toward Vulture Mine; Kruger and Sheppard hold out behind makeshift barricade.

2:00 p.m.   Twenty Indians join party of thirty attackers en route to Date Creek Reservation.

3:00 p.m.   Seven Indians separate from the group and go to Dan O'Leary's ranch to learn from his adopted

	Yavapai son the denominations of the greenbacks they have stolen.
5:00 p.m.	John Nelson reaches the Vulture Mine. Forty-three Indians, including two wounded, arrive at the Date Creek Reservation.
5:15 p.m.	Rescue party of twenty with spring wagon ambulance departs for Culling's Well.
5:36 p.m.	Sunset.
6:02 p.m.	End civil twilight.
7:00 p.m.	Nelson and mine manager John Sexton ride to Wickenburg.
8:00 p.m.	John Nelson alerts Wickenburg to the massacre.
9:30 p.m.	Rescue party collects Kruger, Sheppard, and Nelson's mailbags at Culling's Well. The party heads east to attack site.

November 6, 1871

12:00 a.m.	Pursuit posse departs Wickenburg.
12:30 a.m.	Rescue party collects dead at attack site, departs scene westward, and then south to intersect with the southern route eastward.
1:15 a.m.	Pursuit posse arrives at attack site, beds down.
4:00 a.m.	Rescue party arrives at Wickenburg.
6:29 a.m.	Civil twilight.
6:30 a.m.	Pursuit posse begins investigation of the attack site. Ball's teamsters reach Date Creek army post.
6:55 a.m.	Sunrise.
7:00 a.m.	Pursuit posse finds W. G. Salmon and buries him in a deep cut in the side of a hill.
7:30 a.m.	Pursuit posse departs site and tracks thirty Indians.
9:00 a.m.	Captain Meinhold, Lieutenant Simpson, and twenty enlisted men leave Date Creek for Wickenburg.

10:00 a.m.	The inquest is held.
1:00 p.m.	Bodies removed and buried.
2:30 p.m.	Pursuit posse ceases chase when tracks of twenty Indians join tracks of original party of thirty Indians.
4:00 p.m.	Army arrives in Wickenburg. Captain Meinhold interviews Kruger and Sheppard.
5:34 p.m.	Sunset.
6:00 p.m.	End civil twilight. Pursuit posse returns to Wickenburg.

November 7, 1871

6:30 a.m.	Sunrise. Army column with George Monroe and John Frink ride to attack scene to investigate.
2:00 p.m.	Monroe and Frink ride to O'Leary's ranch.
5:00 p.m.	Army column returns to Wickenburg.
6:00 p.m.	Monroe and Frink return to Wickenburg.

November 8, 1871

| 6:30 a.m. | Captain Meinhold and command departs to cross Bradshaw Mountains, trying to cut trail of Indians who left Date Creek on November 4 for ambush— without success. |

November 9, 1871

Vigilante response averted.

December 1871

Crook begins his investigation. Capt. George H. Burton "on detached service at regimental headquarters" on the general's orders.

January 2, 1872
Captain Burton assigned to the Colorado River Reservation to conduct investigation.

May 31, 1872
Captain Burton returned to duty at regimental headquarters after completing his investigation.

September 7, 1872
General Crook calls for a council with the Apache-Yuma and Apache-Mojave Indians.

September 8, 1872
General Crook attempts arrest of guilty Indians at council. Several Indians are killed and captured.

September 25, 1872
Captain J. W. Mason commanding companies B, C, and K strikes Indians at Burro Creek in the Muchos Cañons. Forty Indians are killed and ten are captured.

December 28, 1872
Captain W. H. Brown with 5th cavalry companies G, L, and M attack "Impenetrable" Indian stronghold in Skeleton Cave, and the entire sib (clan) of Kewevkapaya is destroyed—fifty-seven killed and twenty captured.

March 27, 1873
Captain G. M. Randall with 23rd Infantry attack "Impenetrable" stronghold on Turret Peak. Twenty-three Indians are killed and ten are captured.

April 6, 1873
Cha-Lipun representing the Yavapai tribes surrenders to General Crook.

Winter 1875
Yavapai Indians relocate to the San Carlos Reservation.

Selected Bibliography

Adams, Ramon F. *Western Words: A Dictionary of the Range, Cow Camp, and Trail*. Norman: University of Oklahoma Press, 1944.

Arizona Citizen (Tucson): "The Secretary of War Approves," January 27, 1872; "California Speaks," March 23, 1872; "We reproduce the following . . ." April 6, 1872; "Prescott, May 21," May 23, 1874.

Arizona Enterprise (Florence): August 10, 1878.

Arizona Miner (Prescott): "Stage Line," October 2, 1869; "Auction," October 21, 1871; "The Wickenburg Horror," November 11, 1871; "A Corrected Account of the Massacre," November 18, 1871; "A Report," November 25, 1871; "Colyer's Human Plantation," January 27, 1872; "Misrepresentation of Facts by One of the Survivors," February 17, 1872; "The Hunt for Evidence and the Result," September 14, 1872; "Murder Will Out," September 28, 1872; "More proof . . ." November 9, 1872; "The Apache War," March 22, 1873; "Frightful Deed of Early Days Recalled," May 16, 1916.

Arizona Republic (Phoenix): "Was Ambush Account True?" May 16, 1973.

Army and Navy Journal: "Letter—Kruger to Peckham," January 6, 1872; "Response to previous letter—from Capt. O'Beirne, Lt. Ebstein, Dr. Jones," March 2, 1872.

Barney, James M. "Lighthouse on the Desert." *Arizona Highways,* October 1941.

———. "The Wickenburg Massacre." *Sheriff Magazine,* October 1946.

Basso, Keith H., ed. *Western Apache Raiding & Warfare,* from the notes of Grenville Goodwin. Tucson: University of Arizona Press, 1971.

Beckler, Marion. "He Could Crack a Bullwhip." *Desert Magazine,* August 1950.

Bourke, John G. *On the Border with Crook.* New York: Charles Scribner's Sons, 1891.

Bowen, R. S. "Massacre Avenged." *Arizona Highways,* April 1939.

Brandon, William. *The American Heritage Book of Indians.* Boston: American Heritage Publishing Co., 1961.

Brophy, William A., and Sophie D. Aberle. *The Indian, America's Unfinished Business.* Norman: University of Oklahoma Press, 1966.

Casebier, Dennis G. *Tales of the Mojave Road: Camp Beale's Springs and the Hualpai Indians.* Norco, CA: publisher unknown, 1980.

Cook, James H. *50 Years on the Old Frontier.* New Haven, CT: Yale University Press, 1923.

Daily Alta California: "ARIZONA, Attack by the Indians on the Wickenburg and San Bernardino Stage," November 12, 1871; "Letter from the Governor of Arizona," November 13, 1871; "ARIZONA, Details of the Arizona Stage Robbery and Massacre—Indians Incited by Revenge," November 16, 1871; "The Wickenburg Massacre," November 21, 1871; "The Apaches," November 30, 1871; "The Great Snow Storm," December 16, 1871; "The Indian Question," December 24, 1871; "Stage Massacre—Pursuit of the Indians—The Date Creek Indians Evidently the Murderers," November 25, 1871.

Dorsey, R. Stephen. *Guns of the Western Indian War*. Eugene, OR: Collector's Library, 1995.

Dunlop, Richard. *Wheels West, 1590–1900*. New York: Rand McNally & Co., 1977.

Dyke, William. "A Monument to Early Travel." *Arizona Highways,* May 1937.

Egerton, Kearney. "Wickenburg Massacre Led to Rumor and Suspicions." *Arizona Magazine*. March 4, 1979.

Farish, Thomas Edwin. *History of Arizona*. Phoenix: publisher unknown, 1918.

Fowles, John. *A Short History of Lyme Regis*. Boston: Little, Brown and Company, 1982.

Genung, Dan B. *Death in His Saddlebags: Charles Baldwin Genung, Arizona Pioneer*. Kansas City, KS: Sunflower University Press, 1992.

Haley, James L. *Apaches: A History and Culture Portrait*. Garden City, NJ: Doubleday & Company, Inc., 1981.

Hawkins, Helen B. *A History of Wickenburg to 1875*. Wickenburg, AZ: Helen B. Hawkins, 1950.

Heatwole, Thelma. *GHOST TOWNS and Historical Haunts in ARIZONA*. Phoenix: Golden West Publishers, 1981.

Jackson, Helen Hunt. *A Century of Dishonor: A Sketch of the United States Government's Dealings with Some of the Indian Tribes*. New York: Indian Head Books, 1994.

Josephy, Alvin M., Jr. *The Indian Heritage of America*. Boston: Houghton Mifflin Co., 1968.

Kutac, C. "Where Is the Missing Loot of the Wickenburg Massacre." *Treasure World,* October–November, 1975.

Lauer, Charles D. *Tales of Arizona Territory*. Phoenix: Golden West Publishers, 1995.

Los Angeles *Daily News*: "Mr. Tingley: Attack on Stagecoach by Indians," March 13, 1869; "Passengers for San Francisco," January 9, 1872; "The Wickenburg Massacre—The Survivors Interviewed—Their Thrilling Narrative of the Affair," February 3, 1872; "Passengers for San Francisco," February 13, 1872.

Los Angeles Star: "Passengers for San Francisco," January 9, 1872.

Marrin, Albert. *War Clouds in the West: Indians and Cavalrymen, 1860–1890*. New York: Atheneum, 1984.

McCabe, George F. *The Wickenburg Massacre: A Blessing in Disguise?* Arizona Historical Society. Call #MS603. Unpublished.

McCutcheon, Marc. *The Writer's Guide to Everyday Life in the 1800's.* Cincinnati: Writer's Digest books, 1993.

Miller, Joseph. *The Arizona Story.* New York: Hastings House, 1952.

Murbarger, Nell. "Massacre at Wickenburg." *Frontier Times,* Fall 1959.

National Archives and Records Administration. Depredation Department of the Bureau of Indian Affairs. RG-75, Depredation Book #1, page 220—Claim # 1540-932.

Newell, Gordon, and Joe Williamson. *Pacific Coastal Liners.* New York: Bonanza Books, 1959.

Office of the Adjutant General, War Department. *Decorations of the United States Army, 1862–1926.* Washington, D.C.: U.S. Department of War, 1927.

Panama Star (Panama City, Panama): "The Steamship *Rising Star*. . ." January 27, 1872; "The Pacific Mail Company's Steamship *Alaska* . . ." February 6, 1872.

Press-Enterprise (Riverside, CA): "Stage Robbed! Indians Blamed," June 1, 1997.

Prucha, Francis Paul, ed. *Documents of United States Indian Policy.* Lincoln: University of Nebraska Press, 1975.

Reedstrom, E. Lisle. *Apache Wars: An Illustrated Battle History*. New York: Sterling Publishing Co., 1990.

Roberts, Bill. "Wickenburg Massacre: Still a Whodunit!" *Traveler,* March 1994.

Russell, Carl P. *Guns on the Early Frontiers*. New York: Barnes and Noble Books, 1957.

San Bernardino Guardian: "Another Horrible Murder in Arizona by Indians," November 11, 1871; "Editors Guardian," November 18, 1871; "A Movement Toward Vengeance," November 25, 1871; "The Stage," December 9, 1871; "The Survivors Arrive in San Bernardino," December 30, 1871.

San Bernardino Weekly Times: "Death of Dr. D. J. Evans," March 13, 1896.

Sanders, F. C. S., M.D. *California as a Health Resort*. San Francisco: Bolte and Braden Co., 1916.

San Francisco Chronicle: "Arizona Outrage," November 14, 1871; "Hotel Arrivals," January 11, 1872.

Schmitt, William T. *General Crook: His Autobiography*. Norman: University of Oklahoma Press, 1960.

Schreier, Jim. "The Skeleton Cave Incident." *Arizona Highways,* May 1991.

Schuyler, Walter S. Letter to George W. Schuyler, September 29, 1872. San Marino, CA: Huntington Library, Schuyler Collection.

Schweikart, Larry. *A History of Banking in Arizona*. Tucson: University of Arizona Press, 1982.

Sheridan, Philip H. *Personal Memoirs of Philip Henry Sheridan*. New York: D. Appleton & Co., 1988.

Sheridan, Thomas E. *Arizona: A History*. Tucson: University of Arizona Press, 1995.

Sheridan, Thomas E. and Nancy J. Parezo. *Paths of Life, American Indians of the Southwest and Northern Mexico*. Tucson: University of Arizona Press, 1996.

Sherman, William T. *Memoirs of General William T. Sherman*. Bloomington: Indiana University Press, 1957.

Smith, Bill W. *A Collection of Newspaper Articles, Letters and Reports Regarding the Wickenburg Massacre and Subsequent Camp Date Creek Incident*. Arizona Historical Society. Call# 979.15643. Unpublished.

Stocker, Joseph. "Fate Upsets Hopes for Loot at Wickenburg Stage Massacre." *Arizona Highways*, August 1992.

Sturtevant, William C., ed. *Handbook of North American Indians, Volume 10, Southwest*. Washington, D.C.: Smithsonian Institution, 1983.

Thomas, Alfred B. *Yavapai Indians: A Study of Yavapai History*. New York: Garland Publishing, 1974.

Thrapp, Dan L. *Al Sieber, Chief of Scouts*. Norman: University of Oklahoma Press, 1964.

————. *The Conquest of Apacheria*. Norman: University of Oklahoma Press, 1967.

Truman, Benjamin C. "Knights of the Lash: Old-Time Stage Drivers of the West Coast." *Overland Monthly*. March 1898.

————. *Occidental Sketches*. San Francisco: San Francisco News Co., 1881.

U. S. Government. *Chronological List of Action with Indians, &c., from January 15, 1837 to January 1891*. Fort Collins, CO: Old Army Press, 1979.

Watts, Peter. *A Dictionary of the Old West*. New York: Wing Books, 1977.

Weight, Harold O. "Mystery of the Wickenburg Massacre." *Westways*, March 1967.

White, Jon Manchip. *Everyday Life of the North American Indian*. New York: Indian Head Books, 1979.

Wickenburg Sun: "Do You Remember Early Wickenburg?" Part I, May 19, 1977; Part II, May 26, 1977.

Wooster, Robert. *The Military and United States Indian Policy, 1865–1903*. Lincoln: University of Nebraska Press, 1988.

Worchester, Donald E. *The Apaches: Eagles of the Southwest*. Norman: University of Oklahoma Press, 1979.

R. Michael Wilson has been researching the Old West for fifteen years, following a quarter century as a law enforcement officer in Southern California. He holds an associate's degree in police science, a bachelor's degree in criminology, a master's degree in public administration, and a juris doctorate degree.

Wilson is an active member of the National Outlaw Lawman Association (NOLA) and Western Writers of America (WWA). He has seven history books to his credit, all in his area of interest and expertise—crime and punishment in America's early West. His works represent his philosophy to report "the truth, the whole truth, and nothing but the truth."